Water in a Dry Land

"Margaret Somerville's work defies categorisation: it is ethnography, poetry, research text, and story-telling rolled into one. It is political, humane, and engaging in its treatment of that most serious of subjects: water. The original and embodied methodology will provoke social science researchers and students of social science research to rethink the possibilities for knowledge creation, as well as inspiring new ways of working with co-researchers."

—Miriam Zukas, Adult Education, *Birkbeck, University of London*

"Margaret Somerville and the artist/researchers that she collaborates with have created an inspiring posthuman ethnography about water. *Water in a Dry Land* is a groundbreaking work that challenges readers to fundamentally shift their thinking about water, about research, relations, and the significance of the more-than-human."

—Mindy Blaise, Early Childhood Education,
Hong Kong Institute of Education

"Anyone interested in global water sustainability, Indigenous knowledge, or fresh ways to think about learning, land, and community will find deep inspiration in *Water in a Dry Land*. Margaret Somerville provides here a remarkable model of collaborative innovative research with community. Rendered movingly in story, ritual, and picture, her study overturns convention to reveal striking new insights and sources of knowing for addressing global water crises. But beyond the provocative scholarship here, Somerville's profound personal tale of water draws readers into their own 'thinking through country' that can transform pedagogy and research."

—Tara Fenwick, Education, *University of Stirling*

Water in a Dry Land is a story of research about water as a source of personal and cultural meaning. The site of this exploration is the iconic river system which forms the networks of natural and human landscapes of the Murray-Darling Basin, Australia. In the current geological era of human induced climate change, the desperate plight of the system of waterways has become an international phenomenon, a symbol of the unsustainable ways we relate to water globally.

The Murray-Darling Basin extends west of the Great Dividing Range that separates the densely populated east coast of Australia from the sparsely populated inland. Aboriginal peoples continue to inhabit the waterways of the great artesian basin and pass on their cultural stories and practices of water, albeit in changing forms. A key question informing the book is: What can we learn about water from the oldest continuing culture inhabiting the world's driest continent? In the process of responding to this question a team of Indigenous and non-Indigenous researchers formed to work together in a contact zone of cultural difference within an emergent arts-based ethnography.

Photo essays of the artworks and their landscapes offer a visual accompaniment to the text on the Routledge Innovative Ethnographies Series website, http://www.innovativeethnographies.net. This book is perfect for courses in environmental sociology, environmental anthropology, and qualitative methods.

Margaret Somerville is internationally renowned for her creative and experimental writing and research about place. She is Director of the Centre for Educational Research, which focuses on researching sustainable futures at the University of Western Sydney.

Innovative Ethnographies

Editor: Phillip Vannini

The purpose of this series is to use the new digital technology to capture a richer, more multidimensional view of social life than was otherwise done in the classic, print tradition of ethnography, while maintaining the traditional strengths of classic, ethnographic analysis.

Available

Ferry Tales: Mobility, Place, and Time on Canada's West Coast by Phillip Vannini

Digital Drama: Art Culture and Multimedia in Tanzania by Paula Uimonen

Concrete and Dust: Mapping the Sexual Terrains of Los Angeles by Jeanine Mingé and Amber Lynn Zimmerman

Water in a Dry Land: Place-Learning Through Art and Story by Margaret Somerville

Forthcoming

Geographies of the Imagination: An Art Ethnography of Memories and Reflections on Exile by Lydia Nakashima Deggarod

Beads, Bodies, and Transgressions: A Sensory Ethnography and Commodity Chain Analysis of Public Sex, Labor, and the Carnivalesque by David Redmon

Water in a Dry Land

Place-Learning Through Art and Story

Margaret Somerville

Routledge
Taylor & Francis Group

NEW YORK AND LONDON

Please visit the book's page on the series website at
http://innovativeethnographies.net/water-in-a-dry-land

First published 2013
by Routledge
711 Third Avenue, New York, NY 10017

Simultaneously published in the UK
by Routledge
2 Park Square, Milton Park, Abingdon, Oxon OX14 4RN

Routledge is an imprint of the Taylor & Francis Group, an informa business

© 2013 Taylor & Francis

The right of Margaret Somerville to be identified as author of this work has been
asserted by her in accordance with sections 77 and 78 of the Copyright, Designs and
Patents Act 1988.

Library of Congress Cataloging in Publication Data
Somerville, Margaret.
   Water in a dry land : place-learning through art and story/ Margaret Somerville.
   p. cm. — (Innovative ethnographies)
   Includes bibliographical references and index.
   1. Aboriginal Australians—Australia—Murray River Valley (N.S.W.-S. Aust.)—
Social conditions. 2. Aboriginal Australians—Australia—Darling River Watershed
(Qld. and N.S.W.)—Social conditions. 3. Art, Aboriginal—Australia—Murray
River Valley (N.S.W.-S. Aust.) 4. Art, Aboriginal—Australia—Darling River
Watershed (Qld. and N.S.W.) 5. Indigenous peoples—Ecology Australia—Murray
River Valley (N.S.W.-S. Aust.) 6. Indigenous peoples—Ecology—Australia—
Darling River Watershed (Qld. and N.S.W.) 7. Murray River Valley (N.S.W.-S.
Aust.)—Environmental conditions. 8. Darling River Watershed (Qld. and
N.S.W.)—Environmental conditions. I. Title.
   GN667.M87S65 2013
   306.09944—dc23
   2012027851

ISBN: 978-0-415-50396-9 (hbk)
ISBN: 978-0-415-50397-6 (pbk)
ISBN: 978-0-203-07225-7 (ebk)

Typeset in Caslon, Copperplate, and Trade Gothic
by EvS Communication Networx, Inc.

Printed and bound in the United States of America by
Walsworth Publishing Company, Marceline, MO.

CONTENTS

VIII   CONTENTS

FOREWORD

Statement from Aboriginal Collaborators

Aboriginal philosophy sees learning as a lifelong journey, which evolves in different directions as we explore and discover the world. Sharing our own knowledge and skills not only guides and encourages others' learning, it also widens our own pathway to learning and promotes the giving and receiving of respect.

Badger Bates, Daphne Wallace, and I (Immiboagurramilbun) believe that Margaret Somerville not only understands this philosophy but will always be able to spiritually connect to any place/Aboriginal Country she moves to either through her work or by choice.

Her ability to listen, take note, believe, and express, not only our histories, but also many others in her earlier writings has been achieved through her own knowledge and knowing of herself. Further, the ability to guide and encourage others' learning and also the patience and interest to learn from us, increases our esteem for her. Margaret's ability to incorporate and intertwine our Aboriginal histories with her own experiences, thoughts, and feelings gives proof of the "giving and receiving of respect."

In listening to our different Creation histories, accepting that, though different, all are correct and related, she is innately connected to all the Aboriginal Countries in this beautiful Continent called Australia.

Margaret's capacity to see the most minuscule detail in landscape and its beauty gives further proof of her instinctive spiritual connectiveness to all places/Aboriginal Countries that she visits or lives in.

Immiboagurramilbun

ACKNOWLEDGMENTS

My first acknowledgment must be to Aboriginal peoples all over Australia, the first peoples to occupy and care for this land. From my early experiences in the desert with Pintubi-Luritja women who had not long come into contact with white settlement, to substantial previous research partnerships with Anaiwan, Kamilaroi, Gumbaynggirr, and Gunnai/Kurnai peoples, I have hugely benefited from their knowledge of Country and their teachings. I would like to acknowledge specifically my past collaboration with Gumbaynggirr knowledge holders Tony Perkins, Ken Walker, Gary Williams, and Pauline Hooler as formative in this work.

I especially acknowledge esteemed friend, colleague, cultural mentor, and guide, U'Alayi[1] (Yuwaalaraay) researcher Chrissiejoy Marshall as the reason for the inception of *Water in a Dry Land*. Chrissiejoy Marshall's methodology that we called "thinking through Country" underpins all of this work. We developed this methodology jointly, first for her doctoral thesis, and then for the work we wanted to do about water. We were joined by other artists after Chrissiejoy was incapacitated as a result of a car accident. I am indebted to the contributions of Gomaroi artist/researcher Daphne Wallace, Paakantji artist/researcher Badger Bates, and Yorta Yorta artist/researcher Treahna Hamm, without whom this work would not have been possible. Muruwari doctoral candidate Lorina Barker and

Ngemba knowledge holders Les Darcy and Bradley Steadman also enriched this work with their cultural stories and knowledge.

Many non-Indigenous people have been part of the community of scholars within which this work was nourished and supported. The doctoral group at the University of New England known as the Firey Cottagers, and the Space Place Body Faculty Research Group of Monash University provided friendship, scholarly discussion, and an environment in which new ideas about space, place, and body could grow. It was from within these groups that Chrissiejoy's methodology and my parallel ideas of postmodern emergence came to articulation.

Several research fellows and assistants have been important in shaping the research work and ideas. Phoenix de Carteret was employed as a research fellow on the project for the first 3 years. Her work with the artists was invaluable and her input crucial to the success of the exhibitions at the New England Regional Art Gallery and the Switchback Gallery, Monash University, Gippsland. Rod Forbes, Director of Switchback Gallery, supported the artists in the realization of their curatorial aspirations in those exhibitions. Miriam Potts contributed to the reviewing of literature and to the design and production of the catalogue for the Water in a Dry Land exhibition held at the Albury City Gallery which was supported by the Myer Foundation and the Albury City Council. Sarah Martin contributed photos and text to all of the catalogues, was a continuing source of knowledge and advice, and supported her partner Badger Bates throughout. Sarah was coresearcher with Badger Bates in the Conceptualising Kurnu Paakantji project (Bates and Martin, 2010) which contributed transcript and art material to Badger's chapter. Susan Hampton offered an insightful reading sympathetic to the intention of the work. As a reader and editor of early and later drafts of this book Sue Collins was invaluable in assisting with editing for her extraordinary capacity to work with words in a written text.

I would like to thank Marlene Atleo, University of Manitoba; Michael Corbett, Acadia University; and Aidan Doyle, Newcastle University for their constructive feedback.

Finally, the Australian Research Council, the Myer Foundation, the University of New England, and the Australian Institute of Aboriginal and Torres Strait Islander Studies contributed financial support fundamental for the complex program of research that spanned six years and thousands of kilometers of country.

All proceeds from the sales of this book go to Immiboagurramilbun.

For digital images and story text for this book refer to: http://innovativeethnographies.net/water-in-a-dry-land

PREFACE

Rock and Stone

The reader:

I was looking up into the top of the trees to be able to see it. And I talked about how I have a strong sense of wants about this writing and what I want it to be. I knew that I didn't want it to be about water, I wanted it to be water. It was like being thirsty.

The writer:

I am sitting at the picnic table in Lyndon's Grove, rendered silent, no words. I have spent a month on this writing; two versions of the first chapter, surely this one is better, if not there. What can I say? Searching in my mind for water I return to my last homeplace of twenty years. To the garden of stone on that rocky hill. Dryness of drought, no water.

I cannot give you water, I can only give you rock and stone.

That summer was dry again, every day waiting for rain like the ticking of a clock on a long sleepless night. Teasing gray clouds blow in with the easterly wind and water spits in misty droplets that don't even reach the thirsty ground. The dam is empty and there is no water for the garden so we bucket water from the bath but soft fleshy leaf skin wilts to crackling when roots can no longer find enough moisture.

The frog dam, so noisy after rain that you can't sleep for frog calls, is dry and silent. Inside the big concrete tank under the house, green frogs crowd on a tiny concrete ledge in the dark, for the feel of wet on skin. Only the fine native grasses wave in hot winds, eucalypt trees smell good and strong, and patches of low scrubby ti-tree thrive. At sundown the still air brings a slight smell of damp from the tiny creek that runs at the bottom of the hill.

We live on a rocky ridge above a creek on the northern tablelands of New South Wales. It is a plateau on top of the Great Dividing Range that stands between the east coast and the western plains. High up in the mountains, it is cold in winter and hot in summer. The warm, wet gorge country to the east sometimes sends us good rain. From the west, hot winds blow red dust from the drylands of the great artesian basin. The rain that falls here travels down the mountains to the rivers that flow as surface water across the plains. Some of the rain percolates deep down into the stone and seeps over centuries and millennia into the groundwater that lives in aquifers far below us.

The shallow soil of this land is pale gray and hungry; hungry for nourishment and hungry for water. We live in an ancient land of shallow, fragile soils. Mary White (2000) describes the delicate surface of the desert that protects the topsoil as a skin made of living organisms. When imported farm animals walk with cloven hooves over the land they break this fine skin and the topsoil blows across the land on hot dry winds. Despite the shallow parched soil, outside my bedroom a huge angophora tree spreads its branches. Its leaves are gray-blue mist and its bark rugged and torn. In the late afternoon the setting sun touches the spreading branches with a deep rose pink against a cloudless blue sky.

I garden with rock and stone. The only soil on our land is wedged between rocks of all different sizes and shapes. It is not possible to dig with a fork so I use a crowbar to jimmy up the red-brown rocks. When there are enough rocks I make a low stone wall, fitting the rocks into each other in a slow process of trial and error. It slows me down and somehow fits me into this ground. I sit and look at the form of the rocks and the curves of the ground. The stone wall follows the contours, sitting into the shapes of the land, and inside the curve, the wall holds the thin layer of soil retrieved from this labor. Into this ground I plant sometimes native, and sometimes exotic plants that will weather the harsh dry climate. Lavender, marjoram, and oregano, silver leafed westringias and blue flowered rosemary grow in drifts inside the rock walls. Paths are laid in gravel between the stone walls, and when someone comes to visit their footsteps crunch, crunch on the tiny stones. The gravel is made up of miniature mottled gray, red, and brown pebbles, like the stones of the river where we go to water.

Our favorite water place is a little way to the west at the junction of Booralong Creek and the Gwydir River. The Booralong Creek is all pebbles, river stones, and rocks, rounded and smoothed by the flow of water over centuries. They carry the story of water. In the dry, the creek is slow with still pools where we swim between giant rocks marked with the lines of changing water levels. After rain the creek swells its banks, bubbling and swirling over rock and stone. At the junction where creek meets river, rock and stone give way to sand. There is a little rise with river stones placed in a circle, a fireplace with black coals from the last billy tea. Here we light a fire and sit under the river oaks following the line of a thin golden stream of water that meanders along the sandy riverbed to meet up with other rivers running westwards. Here we are not far from the river's source so there is usually only a small flow of water, sometimes just a trickle. Always it winds its way along the wide golden-sand riverbed, making changing shapes of sandbanks and islands where clumps of river oaks grow, and fish swim in narrow pools along its edges.

Only the vegetable garden is grown with compost, mulch, and water. Because it is impossible to dig, we build no-dig gardens with layers of lucerne (alfalfa) hay, manure collected from nearby paddocks, and whatever compost and organic materials we can scratch together. Baby plants are slipped into a tunnel hollowed out from the hay and filled with compost, then watered and tucked into their beds of straw. Some seasons the garden grows lush and green with lettuce, tomatoes, and basil, silver beet and green beans, yellow capsicums and corn. I think about how hard it is to grow these soft green water-loving plants to eat from our garden and wonder if it would be better to grow the native fruits I have seen flourishing in the dry country. But I have a green soul that comes from another place and longs for water. A firefighter's pump brings water up from the dam at the bottom of the hill but during the first long hot dry summer the dam was emptied. We never saw it full again. The second year we planted in hope but the rain never came.

I decided to call a water dowser to locate groundwater for a bore. The only one we could find lived some two hours away and he arrived with two brass L-shaped rods that he held out, one in each sun-gnarled hand. He started at the rocky ground between the house and fence, holding the rods lightly with their thin metal arms parallel to the ground. When the rods move toward each other, he says, there is a water flow under the ground. He follows his sense of where the water might be, back and forward, and up and down the land, sensing not only the direction of flow, but the depth too. Other dowsers, he tells us, use one Y-shaped twig and hold the single stem lightly with both hands. Willow used to be the traditional choice and divining was called willow-witching. He picks up a Y-shaped eucalypt twig from the ground and shows us that it can work just as well. He hands the branch to me and I imagine I feel the pull of the water held far below the ground within the rock. Ultimately, it is the diviner's body that reads the presence of water through the magnetic fields it creates. My hands are novice, light years from the sensitivity of his, but a different image grows in my body of deep water flowing inside the earth's surface. It is from this place and this moment that the idea for a project about water emerges and Chrissiejoy Marshall sends me in search of water in a dry land.

WATER IN A DRY LAND

Map 1: The Murray-Darling Basin, Australia

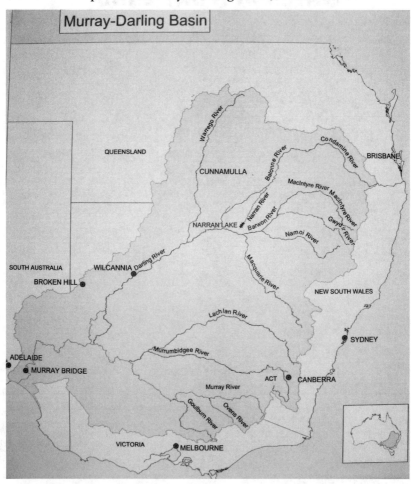

1

MAPPING THE TERRITORY[1]

A map is a story of Country that shapes our relationship to the known world. Maps guide our geographical explorations, near and far, and form the grounding of our thought. They are one of the most naturalized and taken-for-granted ways that our relationship to land is made. In asking how can we think about water differently, *Water in a Dry Land* seeks to create new maps that produce alternative stories and practices. The website connected with this book opens the possibility of thinking spatially and visually through the processes of creating these new tracings across the land.

Global Sustainability and Water

> Making progress towards sustainability is like going to a new country we have never been to before. We do not know what the destinations will be like, we cannot tell how to get there. (Prescott-Allen, 2001, p. 2)

While the concept of sustainability is much criticized for its ubiquitous use and frequent association with maintaining patterns of consumption, it is the tool that global, national, and local organizations have used to initiate authentic action to address planetary problems.

"Sustainability" was placed on the global agenda by the Brundtland Report, *Our Common Future*, delivered to the United Nations in 1987. In that report, sustainable development was defined in anthropocentric terms as "development that meets the needs of the present without compromising the ability of future generations to meet their own needs." This was seen to be especially crucial in relation to environmental limitations; however, the interlinking of the social, the cultural, the environmental, and the economic was emphasized. Population and human resources, food security, species and ecosystems, energy, industry, and the urban challenge of humans in their built environment were considered as essential elements of the sustainability of social and ecological systems. The beginning of the United Nations Decade of Education for Sustainable Development followed in 2005, a culmination of decades of global mobilization for a shift in emphasis toward protecting the environment.

At the time of writing we are no closer to achieving global sustainability. Instead, we have increasing awareness of the momentum of climate change, species loss, risks to food, energy, and water security, and massive global migrations as a result of war and poverty. Scholars in a range of disciplines have taken up Paul Crutzen's term the *Anthropocene* to define a new geological era of human-induced changes to planetary processes: "The Anthropocene represents a new phase in the history of both humankind and of the Earth, when natural forces and human forces became intertwined, so that the fate of one determines the fate of the other" (Zalasiewicz, Williams, Steffen, & Crutzen, 2010, p. 2231). Geologically, they claim, this is a remarkable episode in the history of the planet. Paradoxically, by recognizing human agency and responsibility, this term opens the possibility for emergent responses to more sustainably connect nature and culture, economy and ecology, the natural and human sciences, in order to address escalating planetary problems (Colebrook, 2012).

In a ground-breaking paper, "The Intersections of Biological Diversity and Cultural Diversity," 15 academics from different disciplines and global geographies use the leverage of "the Anthropocene" to map "a novel pathway towards the integration" of ecological and cultural systems (Pretty et al., 2009, p. 105). They argue that previously such systems have been considered separately from each other within different disciplinary boundaries and that we need to link biological and cultural diversity to move beyond the modernist separation of nature and culture. They note substantial evidence supporting the significance of local ecological knowledge expressed as *stories, ceremonies, and discourses*. Local ecological knowledge is constantly in process in relation to the natural world, and can guide a society's actions.

Pretty et al. (2009) argue that language can be thought of as a resource for nature. Cultural knowledge transmitted through language is critical because language links speakers inextricably to landscapes in ways that are often not translatable. Hence, if the language is lost, the cultural knowledge of the landscape is lost with it. Precisely as our knowledge of this connection is advancing, these complex systems linking language, story, landscape, and culture are receding. There is an absence of policy and action on these issues, and dying languages and vast knowledge bases are being lost at rates that are orders of magnitude higher than extinction rates in the natural world. The knowledges that are held in language and story potentially enable humans to live in balance with the environment without the need for "catastrophic learning in the event of major resource depletion."

Water is one of the most urgent and extreme cases of major resource depletion. A panel of international experts states that: "The world is running out of water. It is the most serious ecological and human rights threat of our time" (Barlow, Dyer, Sinclair, & Quiggin, 2008). As we pollute water, we are turning to groundwater, wilderness water, and river water and extracting water faster than it can be replenished (Barlow et al., 2008, p. 2). Approximately 1 billion people lack access to safe drinking water and a 2009 report suggests that by 2030, in some developing regions of the world, water demand will exceed supply by 50%. The problem of water scarcity, however, is not about whether there is enough water, but how we use that water. While indigenous communities all over the world have harvested and managed water in sustainable ways throughout history (Shiva, 2002), during the first major wave of global colonization large dams and irrigation schemes were introduced to extract water to increase agricultural production for profit. The acquisition of colonies was accompanied by "a profound belief in the possibility of restructuring nature and re-ordering it to serve human needs and desires" (Adams & Mulligan, 2003, p. 23).

The practices of restructuring nature intensified during the latter half of the 20th century when new technologies and more productive crops were developed that further depended on harvesting water from most of the major rivers of the world. While these technologies have delivered increases in food production, they have failed in terms of ecological sustainability. Most of the major river systems are now in crisis (Pearce, 2006) and the water crisis is described as "the most pervasive, the most severe, and most invisible dimension of the ecological devastation of the earth" (Shiva, 2002, p. 1).

The work and learning of water has traditionally been the work of community. "In most indigenous communities, collective water rights and management were the key for water conservation and harvesting. By creating rules and limits on water use, collective water management ensured sustainability and equity" (Shiva, 2006, p. 12). The knowledge and practices of managing water sustainably—the sustainable use of water for the production of food and maintenance of all life forms—was learned in families and communities. When millions of people in indigenous communities were displaced by dams and irrigation schemes, the daily work of water to sustain life, and the knowledge associated with that work, was also displaced.

The Nile is an outstanding example of these forces at work. As the longest river in the world, it is shared by 10 African countries: Ethiopia, the Sudan, Egypt, Uganda, Kenya, Tanzania, Burundi, Rwanda, the Democratic Republic of Congo, and Eritrea. The Nile is now a complicated site of water conflict which follows the patterns of displacement of local communities and local knowledge about water (Shiva, 2002, p. 74). The massive construction of dams by the British were "the beginning of the end of the Nile," an end that was accomplished by the Soviet Empire with the building of the Aswan Dam (Schama, 1996, p. 257). The Aswan Dam is described as having displaced 100,000 Sudanese people when it was built in 1958 (Shiva, 2002, p. 75). Most of these discourses about water are stories of irretrievable loss.

Another approach to these dire stories of loss is to seek "a way of looking; of rediscovering what we already have, but which somehow eludes our recognition and our appreciation" (Schama, 1996, p.14). Simon Schama says we do not need "yet another explanation of what we have lost," but "an exploration of what we may yet find" (Schama, 1996, p. 14). Vandana Shiva, too, argues for "a recovery of the sacred and a recovery of the commons" in our relations with water (Shiva, 2002, p. 138). She believes that: "Sacred waters carry us beyond the marketplace into a world charged with myths and stories, beliefs and devotion, culture and celebration; [and that] each of us has a role in shaping the creation story of the future" (Shiva, 2002, p. 139). To do this means creating new stories of water, "we need new versions of these sacred myths: versions that recognize that the sacred rivers may not be so permanent after all" (Pearce, 2006, p. 350).

Water in Australia: The Murray-Darling Basin

As the driest inhabited continent on earth (Rose, 2007), Australia uses more water per head of population than any other country in the world (Sinclair, 2008). Extreme climate variations over the last several decades are believed to have been produced by global warming effects. In 2005, the year this program of research began, Australia had been in the grip of the most severe drought in the continent's recorded history (Somerville, 2008b).[2] The 13-year drought brought global attention to the region in eastern Australia known as the Murray-Darling Basin, referred to in some accounts as "the nation's food basket."

A typical map of the Murray-Darling Basin shows the coastline of the island continent now known as Australia, the boundary lines of states, the names of the major capital cities, and the major rivers with their English names. This conventional map of the Murray-Darling Basin produces an imaginary that parallels the predominance of scientific, positivist inquiry and discourses in relation to water in the Murray-Darling Basin. Despite massive resources spent on scientific research to analyze the extent and nature of the ecological problem, we do not know how to transform the way we think, and consequently act, in relation to water.

The Murray-Darling Basin covers approximately one seventh (14%) of the total area of Australia, contains two thirds of the country's irrigated lands, and produces 40% of the country's agricultural output, valued at $10 billion a year. It includes almost the whole of inland south-east Australia, extending across parts of five states: the Australian Capital Territory, Queensland, New South Wales, Victoria, and South Australia. Each state is a separate governmental jurisdiction. The Basin catchment area lies west of the Great Dividing Range that marks the division between the highly populated and well-watered eastern seaboard and the drier, sparsely inhabited inland. Both ground and surface water flow west from the Great Dividing Range into the Basin. The network of rivers and their tributaries begins in the headwaters of the Balonne and Condamine Rivers in Queensland and flows down through the Narran, Culgoa, and Bokhara Rivers to the Darling, eventually joining the Murray, Australia's longest river. The Murray River travels through several lakes to enter the sea in large estuarine wetlands in South Australia.

In 1990 the Murray-Darling Basin (MDB) Ministerial Council launched a strategy of "integrated catchment management," in response to the declining health of the system of water. Over 10 years later, they reported that water quality and ecosystem health were continuing to decline (MDB, 2001, p. 2). Significantly, they emphasized "the importance of people in the process of developing a shared vision and acting together to manage the natural resources of their catchment" (MDB, 2001, p. 1). A scoping study on Aboriginal involvement in the proposed initiatives found a "chasm between the perception of the available opportunities for involvement and the reality experienced by Aboriginal people" (Ward, Reys, Davies, & Roots, 2003). The study found, "Aboriginal people are concerned and angry about the decline in health of the Murray-Darling Basin" (Ward et al., 2003, p. 21) and that there was a strong case for involving Aboriginal people because of the "collective and holistic nature of Aboriginal people's concerns about the natural environment and their Country" (Ward et al., 2003, p. 29). The most significant barrier to Aboriginal involvement was identified as a "lack of respect and understanding of Aboriginal culture and its relevance to natural resource management" (Ward et al., 2003, p. 8).

The situation continued to decline. The Murray River was described as dying in 2007 due to decreasing flows of water downstream (Sinclair, 2008) and the Darling was reduced to a series of toxic puddles in some places, with towns threatened with loss of water supply. The Narran Lake, a Ramsar listed wetlands of international significance in the middle of the system of waters was on the verge of irreversible decline (Thoms, Markwort, & Tyson, 2008). The Murray-Darling Basin Commission proposed further draining of wetlands, building more dams and complex water trading schemes to address urgent and highly contested needs for water. Flooding rains in 2011, and again in 2012, brought some relief to the urgency, but even then when the federal government decided to buy back land and irrigation licenses, there were angry and violent protests. The question remains unchanged: How can we transform our stories and practices of water in this old dry land, and indeed globally?

Different Maps and Forms of Knowledge Production

Aboriginal people continue to inhabit all of the lands and waterways of the Murray-Darling Basin but the stories and practices through which they have survived since the last Ice Age are largely unknown in mainstream Australian culture. The processes through which this knowledge might become visible have not been developed because of fundamental paradigm differences between Aboriginal understandings of Country, and Western knowledge frameworks. A map of the Aboriginal languages of the Murray-Darling Basin offers a potential beginning point for new understandings.

Australia had over 200 distinct Aboriginal languages with around 600 different dialects at the time of white settlement. A number of linguists have mapped the distribution of these languages. Most notably Norman Tindale traveled throughout Australia to develop the first maps from extensive linguistic research and David Horton produced the most recent digital versions from archival research (see AIATSIS website). Even though these maps of the territory of Aboriginal languages are already artifacts of print literacy, they still allow us to begin to imagine the possibility of a different reality. The portion of Horton's map labeled the Riverine Language Group shows 40 patches of different colors of variable sizes and shapes outlined with an irregular line of dark pink to indicate their linguistic coherence. The pink line delineates the territory of the Riverine Language Group which overlaps almost exactly with the map of the Murray-Darling Basin. The fuzzy lines where the different patches of color meet and merge indicate that language territory boundaries are determined by complex ecological and human relations and negotiations.

The stark difference between the standard map of the Murray-Darling Basin and the map of the Aboriginal Riverine Language Group draws attention to the difference between positivist scientific research about natural phenomena and qualitative studies about people and their relationships to place and to each other. While both make important contributions to our understanding and knowledge of the world, qualitative research is grounded in an understanding of "the other" originating historically in ethnographic research.

Ethnography is at the heart of qualitative research as method. Derived from the Greek *ethnos*, meaning people, and *grapho* meaning to write, it fundamentally concerns the relationship between the study of peoples and the ways we write about them. Based in anthropology as a disciplinary field, however, ethnography emerged in parallel to the colonization of many indigenous peoples of the world. By the mid-1980s critiques were mounting about the colonizing nature of anthropological knowledge, and the impossibility for the colonizer to represent the lives of the colonized other. In response to the recognition of complicity in the processes of colonization, a fundamental critique of ethnographic practice emerged. The "death of ethnography" was announced.

The tradition of auto/ethnography sprang from this response. The ethnographic study of the self produced a wide array of diverse texts of self-experience. The tradition of auto/ethnography has yielded important methodological innovations in storytelling and art-based practice, but has been criticized for its inward looking focus. In auto/ethnography there seems to have been a retraction from the necessary, difficult, and challenging work of understanding the mutual entanglement of self and other in the constitution of subjectivity. The act of inhabiting the slash between auto, the self, and ethno, the other, is one of the most difficult things to do in research.

Another possibility is opened by researcher "reflexivity"—acknowledging, interrogating, and disrupting the presence of the researcher "I." Enduring questions for researcher reflexivity are: Where am I in this research and how do my actions as a researcher shape the knowledge made possible through this research and its representations? As a female, Antipodean, third generation Scottish immigrant, I research in the context of the relations between Indigenous and non-Indigenous knowledge systems in Australia. My research involves place, body, collaborations, and partnerships in a contact zone of cultural difference, and the necessity to work across disciplinary boundaries and research paradigms. I am particularly interested in the moments and movements of translation in research practice—from body and country to representation and writing. This has pushed questions of representation to the limits of language, and beyond. An ethnography of Country stretches into new possibilities for thinking visually and spatially.

Language, Story, and Storylines

The notion of language as shaping our relationship to land is fundamental to this work. "Language not only records people's empirical observations of the countryside, it offers some evidence, like bubbles on the surface, tracing out the creative ways people have tried to make sense out of their relationships with their environment" (Goodall, 2002, p. 37). Language and people are mutually constituted in place: "Landscape does not just shape language; the land itself is transformed by words" (Bonahady & Griffiths, 2002, p. 6). The concept of language and story includes the verbal expressions of scientists, politicians, agriculturalists, as well as novelists, poets, and so on. In Australia, for example, Sinclair describes stories about the Murray River as participating in a "broader cultural and political narrative of technological and agricultural progress." Such stories are shaped by "the vision of a barren land being made productive; of a silent and timeless place being transformed and brought into history by the energy of an industrious and resourceful society" (Sinclair, 2001, p. 43). Pastoralists' dominant stories of land in the Murray-Darling Basin have been described as "inescapably adversarial" (Griffiths, 2002, p. 240) because of the harsh dry conditions that European settlers found so confronting.

I extend the concept of *story* to embrace the expressions of visual artists, film, and performance, drawing from Australian Indigenous practices of story. An Aboriginal story incorporates song, music, dance, body painting, and performance, all intersecting powerfully in a particular place through ceremony (Somerville & Perkins, 2010). Contemporary Australian Aboriginal art draws from the intersection of these forms in ceremony and Country. Every knowledge framework, discipline, and artistic modality has its own forms and genres of place stories.

Changing our relationship to places means changing the stories we tell; "If human beings are responsible for place making, then we must become conscious of ourselves as place makers and participants in the sociopolitical process of place making" (Gruenewald, 2003, p. 627). The analytical strategy of storylines, as developed in feminist poststructuralism, can be used to analyze how stories function to shape places: "A storyline is a condensed version of a naturalized and conventional cultural narrative, one that is often used as the explanatory framework of one's own and others' practices and sequences of action" (Sondergaard, 2002, p. 191).

The concept of storylines in feminist poststructuralism has parallels with the Aboriginal concept of storylines. The storyline within each framework is understood as the skeleton of a significant cultural narrative structure that informs patterns of thought and action. The fundamental difference is that Aboriginal storylines are always connected to the land. Storylines link places across the landscape where significant events in the creation stories of the ancestors took place. Each of these places is a site where ceremony is performed for the well-being of Country and its people. In taking up this doubled meaning, the concept of storylines can be used to seek out previously invisible place stories or to generate new stories about place.

Thinking through Country

The research which underpins *Water in a Dry Land* began in collaboration with U'Alayi language speaker Immiboagurramilbun (Chrissiejoy Marshall) who grew up on the Narran Lake in the middle of the Murray-Darling Basin. Chrissiejoy came to me as a doctoral student to research the process of developing a conflict resolution package with a number of Aboriginal communities across New South Wales. The methodology of her research evolved directly from her relationship to her birth country of the Narran Lake. After struggling with academic thought and language we worked out that in order to make any knowledge claims at all, she had to think through Country, the specific country of the Narran Lake. She developed her methodology using a combination of visual, oral, and written forms. In performing her methodology Chrissiejoy presented a painting and an accompanying oral account that structured and informed each cluster of meanings, or chapters of her thesis.

In presenting the paintings Chrissiejoy said: "There is no one word in any Aboriginal language that I can find for the term 'art,' which is lucky for me, who not for one moment considers myself an artist.... It is far more important that the paintings actually describe to the viewer the information that I am telling." For Chrissiejoy, her paintings are a medium to express and communicate complex ideas, as much for herself as for her viewers.

> Aboriginal Art has only become Art in the last 200 plus years. What anthropologists and others have described as crude and unsophisticated art, was actually Aboriginal pictorial reflections simply for the passing on of knowledge, so that the listener or learner could visually grasp the concept or subject matter being given. Similarly, that which is now described as dance, song and ceremony was (simplistically put) much more a way of passing on information including history, lore and laws, than the recreational pursuits that are presently ascribed. The symbols and drawings described by those anthropologists and historians actually constitute a complex code of interaction that continually reflects on Aboriginal cosmology, philosophies, spirituality, history and laws that have been used for thousands and thousands of years (Immiboagurramilbun, 2005).

Chrissiejoy's paintings draw on a tradition where a multiplicity of art forms including dance, song, and ceremony, intersect in the ongoing creation of self and Country. According to her reflexive analysis, they draw on ancient cosmology, spirituality, history, and laws, while simultaneously being a contemporary form with contemporary meanings. She is aware of generating knowledge in the context of a Western academic institution and her paintings and stories emerge in the contact zone between these two knowledge traditions. They are an example of new knowledge being formed rather than old knowledge being retold.

In her presentation she created a carefully orchestrated performance in conversation with her non-Indigenous audience using her paintings, oral storytelling, U'Alayi and Erinbinjori language, and the act of translation. Each of these elements made meaning in relation to each other part of the performance. She produced a DVD from her scripted conversation and images of her paintings, which she insisted on keeping separate from the written thesis document. By keeping them separate Chrissiejoy was able to move between the paintings, the oral storytelling, and the written word to articulate what otherwise would have been unsayable and unknowable in her academic writing. When we incorporated this methodology into our collaborative work we named it "Thinking through Country."

In parallel to Chrissiejoy's methodology of thinking through Country I developed a methodology I called, for want of a better name, *postmodern emergence* (Somerville, 2007). I use this term to express the emergent nature of knowledge production, which I believe is absent and under theorized in most research accounts. In articulating postmodern emergence I drew on the processes that I had observed in so many of my students who came from different knowledge frameworks. I wanted to articulate a generalized approach that would assist in shaping their alternative approaches, so that each individual did not have to start from scratch every time. In postmodern emergence I emphasize the importance of a stance of unknowing, and the irrational, messy, embodied, and unfolding nature of our participation as bodies in the "flesh of the world." This necessarily involves us in a reciprocal relationship with objects and landscapes, weather, rocks and trees, sand, mud and water, animals, and plants. In this ontology, subjectivities are dynamic, always forming in relation to each other, and in relation to the inanimate materials and technologies such as stone, wood and clay, pencils, crayons, brushes, paints, computers, words, and paper that we use to create meaning.

Postmodern emergence shaped the research design of our collaborative work to be responsive to the emergent nature of relationships between people and between people and places. It allowed the research to evolve, to include creative forms, other Aboriginal artist researchers and other places, as it traveled with the waters of the Murray-Darling Basin. Each time a story, an artwork, or a piece of writing was produced constituted a pause, a temporary stopping place in an iterative process of representation and reflection. In this way, each instance of representation did not aim at stasis but had its own truth in which meaning is formed relationally, dynamically and intertextually. Together we (per)formed our becoming-other to ourselves in a process of mutual entanglement.

Mutual Entanglement

The mutual entanglement of indigenous and non-indigenous peoples in matters of water and country is fundamental to this research. The concept of mutual entanglement originates from an ethnographic study of exchange between indigenous people and colonizers in the Pacific Islands. It was observed that the exchange of cultural objects was reciprocal, that both colonizers and colonized gave and received objects from each other's cultures. In giving and receiving objects from another culture, part of that cultural other is incorporated into the self. Through this act the ontological self is transformed.

This notion can be further understood through the idea of the transitional object. Studies of young babies have shown that in the process of becoming a separate being in the world, an object becomes imbued with the characteristics of the infant's relationship with the mother's body. This object, in its specific material sensory form, supports the transition of the infant to become a separate being, the time of insertion of the self into the symbolic order of language. Through the transitional object, however, a part of oneself always remains in an embodied connection to the whole, to the mother, and to the prelanguage state.

In this collaborative research the artworks functioned as transitional objects. At the most simple level they were offered as gifts, becoming literally incorporated into the other through their presence in the other's world. These gifts were a way of bridging different understandings, relationships, and knowledges of Country and water. They expressed our growing relationships and the intermingling of knowledges. At times the art also actually represented the nature of mutual entanglement of Indigenous and non-Indigenous people in Country.

Gomaroi artist Daphne Wallace's painting of a satellite image of the Narran Lake maps the concept of mutual entanglement in visual form. In a bird's eye view of Country, the land around the Narran Lake is constructed with differently colored squares of cultivation—the green, gold, red, brown of cotton, sorghum, pasture, plowed ground. Traversing and disrupting these geometrical divisions marking the private ownership of land, the lake and the waters that feed into it wind in and out, through and across the squares of divided country. The large oil painting has a textural and sensual surface that adds another dimension to its meanings. The water shimmers with a shiny white, representing the energy the life-giving water brings to the land. The patches of different colors are, in part, produced by the water of irrigation. Both water and land are marked by cultural stories, with the water carrying the symbols of Aboriginal water stories, less visible than the geometrical divisions of land into exclusive private space.

Mutual entanglement is not only about the intertwining of peoples but expresses the intertwining of selves in place: "Place is thus remarkable as an unwindable spiral of material form and interpretive understanding" (Gieryn, 2000, p. 471). This definition of place echoes the twisting spiral of the DNA molecule as a visual expression of an embodied reality. In this understanding of place, all of the material qualities of a place, including the shapes of the land, are mutually shaped by human actions, including their representational processes.

The divisions of land into geometrical portions with boundaries marked by fences, for example, is a representational process that shapes both the land and our relationship to it: "The story I am part of is one thread of a global web of stories about displacement and resettlement, dispossession and environmental degradation, and will be familiar to thousands of people in rural Australia" (Findlay, 2007, p. 311).

The processes of mutual entanglement played out in similar ways throughout our work together, the thread of water winding in and out of our mutual concerns. In the beginning we each operated as individual selves, bringing our individual histories, experiences, and knowledge to the collective process. At times it seemed impossible as we wrestled with the impacts of colonization and our different positioning around the colonial divide. As our work matured, however, we grew together in many ways, so that in the transcripts of our later conversations it is almost impossible to tell who is speaking which words. Narratives are constructed by multiple voices, each offering a part of the overall story. This was represented in the making of art as well, with the artists responding to each other's artworks, stories, and Country in their own art making.

Deep Mapping

It is through the method of deep mapping that we materialize our mutual work of mapping water country in this ethnographic research. Deep mapping is an adaption of cultural mapping techniques developed in collaboration with Gumbaynggirr people on the midnorth coast of New South Wales (see Somerville & Perkins, 2010b).[3] In deep mapping we use road maps to mark story places simultaneously with the digital recording of oral stories. The roads and English language place names are then removed using Photoshop software and the story places are replaced on the empty map with story text and photos. The method is a representational reversal of the processes of colonization. Contemporary, historic, and creation story places are mapped in this way, creating new multilayered image/maps of Country that incorporate the deep time of creation in the present.

Intensive language work, especially language work that involves recovery of "lost" language and meanings, is a part of the deep mapping process. In such language work, complex encoded information recorded in sacred oral stories is linked back to Country, to the actual physical terrain where events happened in a storyline of creation. Through this language work, deep time stories are connected to a contemporary present in the form of new visual images, making alternative "maps" of country. When language, story, and country are reconnected, storylines become songlines again and Country can once again be sung into (well-)being.

Deep mapping evolved to another level in *Water in a Dry Land* with the use of contemporary art techniques by the Aboriginal artists to map their relationships to Country and water. These relationships were represented in a variety of forms, depending on the media, the country, and the artist concerned. Badger Bates's black and white lino print, *Iron Pole Bend, Wilcannia* is a good example of these artworks as alternative maps of country. This print, which I write about in detail in chapter 7, functions entirely differently from typical maps of the Murray-Darling Basin produced by state and federal water authorities. A fundamentally different and culturally sophisticated relationship to space, place, and country is represented in the spatiality of *Iron Pole Bend*.

The print depicts a particular bend in the Darling River, too local, too insignificant to appear on any road map. For Badger it is a map of home and (water) country. The print is named after an iron pole that was inserted into the river bank by white settlers, a mark of colonization that significantly does not appear in the image. Only its written English name contains the traces of colonization. The dominant feature in the print is the movement and meeting of the waters, lines of force and energy produced from the mouths of the Ngatyi, the Rainbow Serpents. The waters flow into and out of the print, unconstrained by its square black and white frame. In the river are all the creatures that the river gives life to and which gave food to Paakantyi people—fish, mussels, yabbies, and shrimp. Penetrating into the waters are the dreamtime creatures of the brolga, kangaroo, and goanna. They travel in from far away and their songlines connect beyond this place.

The sky is depicted above in a transition to a more Western landscape aesthetic. It is a black night sky with a white moon and a black shape of emu formed within the white stars of the Milky Way.

Starting with White

Writing from the visual images of the artworks did not take shape immediately in constructing this work. When I began writing I drew on the as yet unformed images from my first journey to the Narran Lake. The images from this trip had lodged in my body but remained unarticulated until I began with white. The first stopping place, a white brick motel in Moree with white towels fluttering on drying lines and white cars parked in rows had gathered into a few sparse words, a stark beginning point for this writing. In starting with white, I take up my responsibility as the choreographer of this ethnographic work to write the book as my own creative practice of placemaking. To begin with white is to face the blank page, a space without inscription. It is a stance of writing place as ontological uncertainty.

Place is known through the senses, through the body, and the subtle pedagogies of layered storying which every place contains. Writing about place is an ontological act, producing the self at the same time as writing the words. It is predicated on unwinding the spiral of "material form and interpretative understandings or experiences" to enable new possibilities to come into being.

There is no map for the country of this writing. It is always being at the edge of territory, it is like being on the edge of the cliff, always shaping new words to make a bridge into that space. Each word is thrown into the empty space, the abyss of the white page, and each forms a link, ever so tenuous and fragile, that holds the body of the writer as she moves there.

Map 2: White

2
WHITE[1]

To drive to the western plains is like going to another country. Mount Yarrowyck marks the boundary, the place beyond which I enter unknown territory. Over the years my visits to Mount Yarrowyck have become something of a pilgrimage. There is a parking lot on the road that leads out west, not far past the bridge over the Booralong Creek. From there a track goes to a rock art site halfway along the western side of the mountain, a walk through trees and huge lichen-laced rocks. High above an eagle circles over steep walls of bare rock that reach into an indigo sky. At the end of the track I sit close to the small rock overhang marked with symbols of bird tracks and hand-prints in white and red ochres. They say that only the Noolungurra, the old clever man, can make these marks on the rock. He goes to the cave at night under the waning moon when the white ochre shines. The bird prints are the tracks of the plains turkey, the people of the western plains, the people that live beyond my country. I have been to this special place with Aboriginal people from Armidale over many years and I have heard their stories. An old Aunty says, "Different tribes used to go out there and have a meeting sort of thing, y'know, join together and a lot of them traveled. And there was other sites just over on the other mountain at each point."[2]

Over the years I have learned more about this rock art site. It is part of a complex pattern of ceremonial gathering places linked to the river and to the three nearby mountains. There are women's and men's special places and other art sites. The river gave the people sustenance for large gatherings and the rocks held the meaning of their ceremonies. They said that people from the western plains met here with the people from the east. The most significant ceremonies were held at these edge places that mark the boundaries of Country and language. Boundaries are known from within one's identity in Country, through stories, through relationships and connections. My Gumbaynggirr friends from the east coast told me that when crossing a boundary into another country you have to call out in language to the spirits of that country:

> You're alright to go anywhere as long as you can talk for yourself. If you don't talk you probably will see something. "Yaam guumunbu ngaya yirringin ngaya yilaaming, spirit, don't come here."

But I do not know the language or the country beyond this place. I drive on because Chrissiejoy has sent me to learn her country first hand. I begin the trip with maps, road maps of country, but there is no single map that is big enough to show all the places we are to travel. There are road maps of every state, but the spatial map of this trip crosses three state boundaries. Only the big map of the Murray-Darling Basin, stretching across four states, linked to five capital cities, is big enough. But that big map has none of the detail that we need to find our way. How does one learn Country? It is the body, "the flesh of the world" (Merleau-Ponty, 1962) that is missing from these maps. And in this country all of the places have been crisscrossed with new roads, new stories, and new language. There is nothing to bridge my movement into this country. I have no map of this territory, no name to call out to the spirits to enter this unknown place, only a big white university car that follows the roads heading west.

There is not much sense of traveling over the edge of the mountains and falling into the gorges that marks my usual journey driving east toward the sea. The road down the western slopes is slow and gentle. Only in one spot, just before we get to the first town, Bingara, there is an edge place with a lookout that reveals a vast flat plain stretching as far as I can see. The road winds back and forth along our same Gwydir River that is heading westwards with us. All the way the sky is big, with banks of clouds. Down from the mountains the road opens out onto endless flat plains. Huge road trains with up to three long trailers own the road and balls of cotton fluff blow along yellow dirt edges in their wake. In the middle of the road a newly dead echidna lies on her back, soft belly and pouch exposed, the first of many road kills. Her hands are like my hands, fingers and palm facing upwards baring tender pink fleshy pads. The body is cold but not yet stiff so it flops when I lift her by the arms to avoid the spines and place her in a pocket of prickly bushes beside the road. The quality of echidna surprises me, recalling the shock when Patsy, my Aboriginal friend, brought a plate to the table for our lunch with an echidna lying similarly, tender palms exposed.

The first stop, Moree, is described as the "Gateway to the Outback" at the Tourist Information Centre. The brochures say that it is the "Artesian Spa Capital of Australia." Streets are lined with motels for people visiting the huge public baths complex and some that advertise their own small pools of artesian water. We find one of these small motels on the highway going north. It is a white concrete block construction with rows of small square rooms. Outside each room a parking place is set slightly at an angle to fit the rows of cars. In the middle of the courtyard the white sheets and towels of the motel are drying in bright sunlight. I unpack the car and spend the afternoon in the Moree library, following the history of the artesian waters.

Looking up catalogues, searching the literature, compiling, collecting, sorting information, are all deeply satisfying. I collect all the papers, maps, photos, writings, and material artifacts of the research and carry them with me in a box. But what holds the experience of Moree and the artesian waters is the undoing I experience when I leave the university and let go of a self that is bound by all of that. I record this in my journal in body/place writing. This writing originated in a certain exhaustion of the self, of logics, of academia, a dis-ease. I began a process of bodywork in which images lodged in the body emerged through massage, the touch of skin on skin. In that space between self and other, the movement of finger on skin, the massage practitioner articulates a knowing through touch. The touched body responds with images that exist in the body before words, and draws them into articulation. Not sense making, but nonlogic word attachment from multiple sites of the sensing body, the space between self and other, self and world.

In Moree the undoing of self is held in the image of white sheets and towels drying on racks in the square courtyard of the Dragon and Phoenix Motel. The herringbone phalanx of white cars parked outside square white motel rooms, always moving on their way to somewhere, nowhere; white skin of body floating in clear artesian waters. These gather onto other images as I move through country: echidna lying dead on road, amputated trees in cages, the curved line of the horizon, the pattern of stars in the great expanse of the black night sky, silver water dancing over rock and stone. All of this is part of a complex pattern that I want to enter. Beginning with white.

White I

White
is not a colour
I usually
write.

The white history of Moree could be told through the story of the artesian waters. The drilling for the first bore to access the artesian water on the North West Plains was begun in 1893 to provide water for cattle on a new stock route to Boggabilla. The bore in nearby Moree was begun two years later in 1895 but was completed first. Water dowsers could tell them where to drill but they never knew how far down they would have to go, nor how much water a bore would yield. The long tedious process of drilling the bore with 40 foot long wooden poles was fueled by a steam engine which burned hundreds of tons of timber felled from the surrounding flood plains. The machinery, developed in Canada, was carted around the countryside by camels imported from Afghanistan. In 1895 the Moree bore opened with a fanfare when locals could "take the waters" from a "standing pipe" with a flow of 607,247 gallons of water per day.

The first official bore baths were opened in 1898 in a small timber building with a single basin managed by Mrs. Lottroph. Next came the "ladies basin" where Miss Anastasia Kane began her 30 years of service in 1913. By 1930 it was deemed necessary to regulate the bodies at the baths:

> It is compulsory for you to have a shower and use soap before entering the basins. Patients will readily see that this rule tends to keep up the standard of hygiene for which the baths are noted. Cuspidors are provided around the basin and it is an offence for any person to expectorate on the floor or in the basin.
>
> The Council will not permit any person to use the public basins who may appear to be suffering from any skin eruption, broken skin, boils, or an other affection [sic].
>
> The cubicles are constantly cleaned and scrubbed and patients are requested not to place their boots on the seats.

A part of the history of the regulation and control of bodies was the exclusion of Aboriginal bodies from the public baths. In February 1965 a busload of Aboriginal activists and their sympathizers from Sydney University, led by Charles Perkins, arrived in Moree. The object of the Freedom Riders was to expose the unacceptable conditions under which Aboriginal people lived across rural New South Wales. They successfully pressured the Council to allow a party of local Aboriginal children to enter the baths, but as soon as they left another group of Aboriginal children was refused entry. When the Freedom Riders returned to protest again, a violent clash erupted and the Baths were temporarily closed. Shortly after, the principle of open access to all was won. A young Aboriginal woman at the library tells me her grandfather still has a copy of the photo of police taking Charlie Perkins out of the baths.

On Thursday morning at the baths four ladies in brightly colored clothes are chatting on plastic seats beside the pool. A few people, mainly men who look middle European, are in the water. I ease myself into the hot water and wait for a favored spot at the jet. An old Aboriginal woman sits on her plastic chair next to the pool with a gray-haired man beside her talking loudly to another in the water.

"They complained to the Council about how I kicked me dog," he yells above the noise of jets and people, "yer can do what yer like in yer own fuckin' backyard." The brightly colored ladies get into the water in the corner near the little jets and chat noisily in Italian. A small Japanese woman walks around the pool then gets in gingerly at the steps. The dog-kicking man moves over to the big jets beside the laughing ladies and says "Arriverderci Roma?" and they nod "yes," knowing he means to say are they speaking in Italian. They stop chatting and scan the rest of the pool and one of them asks if they are bothering me. "No," I say, "I love all the talk." "The gossip?" she asks. "Yes," I say. "Did you all know each other before you came here?" "For a long time in Sydney," she replies, "but this is my first time here."

That night, in the Dragon and Phoenix Motel with its Vietnamese restaurant, we meet two tall dark men from Arimathaea. They tell us they are among the very few Arimathaean speakers left in the world. They explain that not many people know the story of their people and their language. So they tell us the story of Joseph of Arimathaea. Joseph, they say, was a secret disciple of Jesus, not one of the twelve named and storied followers. When Joseph heard the news of Jesus' death, he went immediately to Pontius Pilate and asked for the body of Jesus. Pilate, reassured by a centurion that the death had taken place, gave Joseph permission to go to the body. In preparation Joseph bought fine linens and spices and traveled to Golgotha where Jesus' body hung from the cross. There, assisted by Nicodemus, he took the body down, washed and prepared the body with myrrh and aloes, and wrapped it in fine white linen.

The ritual preparation of the body in death was traditionally women's work, they say, but for Joseph of Arimathaea it was a very personal expression of his love and devotion. When his work was done, he placed Jesus' body in his own burial place, a tomb carved from rock in his garden. He sealed the tomb with a massive stone. This was the place, they tell us, where Mary Magdalene found the stone rolled aside and the body of Jesus gone. The white linens remained in the rock tomb, marked by the blood of the body they held. We fall into silence after this big story, each of us losing ourselves in the wash of warm water and the worlds that have opened before us.

Waking up in the motel the next morning, there is another story of the body. Last night I felt the cool cotton sheets against the heat of my body, skin smooth and soft from relaxing in the hot pool. Today I begin the day with yoga. A tiny space on the motel room floor is just big enough for my yoga mat. It is difficult to stretch out the body after a long spell of hard work at a computer. The stretching is a discipline of stillness, of bringing the body here into this present. After yoga I hop back into the hot pool for some more unwinding when I notice the spot. On the back of my hand there has appeared at some time in the past few weeks, a round, raised lumpy red-brown spot. At first I thought it was a burn but then it dawned on me that it wasn't going away, it was round, not burn shaped, and slightly itchy from time to time. I have looked at it frequently since I left work to begin this trip, the time when these body things can enter into consciousness.

I think of my brother who died from a malignant melanoma. He was only in his 40s. It was a horrible death from secondary melanoma tumors in his brain. He denied that he was dying so I couldn't say goodbye until he was almost unconscious. When I was finally allowed to visit he was lying in a special high bed in a bay window looking out to the sea from his home on the headland. Hollowed out, skin and bone, eyes sunken deep into the bony skull of his eye sockets, he was almost unrecognizable as the handsome sport-loving brother he had been. I told him I loved him and held his hand, talking softly to him about our lives, his big sister. His eyes flickered as if in a smile, and he squeezed my hand just a little, almost indiscernible, that was all.

The process of bringing the body into focus, my body, and allowing images to emerge is one of de-authoring myself in order to learn this country. There seem to be two simultaneous and equally significant processes in coming to know something new through this research. One is a rational process of logic and ordering and the other is of coming to know through the body, a necessary unraveling of the self, of certainty and prior knowledge. This unraveling I access through body/ place writing, through the images that were called up on that first trip, that come from a deep place within.

Water and cleanliness, white hands, blotchy white skin with a new black spot, melanoma? Brother dying, the problem of white skin, sun and belonging in this land. Am I going to die? What a silly question this is, of course I am, but not yet, and probably not from this spot. Each time I wake in the night I feel the shape of the slightly rough skin and sense from the inside if it is itchy. In the first light I look to see if it has changed but it mostly looks the same, a round dark red circle, about the diameter of a pencil on the outside edge of my right hand. The skin on the back of my hands is sun damaged, wrinkled, and older looking than it should be, spotted with freckles and sun spots. I have been a gardener for many years and my hands are marked by the intense sunlight. That is the thing about skin cancers, they are directly related to our relationship with the environment. My fair Scottish skin doesn't belong here. In Scotland the light was much softer, gentler, hazier, quite different from the bright clear sunlight of this place. The quality of light is especially bright and intense out here in the wide open spaces of the west.

My Dad also had a melanoma on his back that made a big scar when they cut it out. He split the scar open by exercising too vigorously when the stitches were just out and they had to stitch it up again. He said all his goodbyes at the time, 30 years ago, and has had two more melanomas removed since. Then just as I begin writing about water in a dry land he too is diagnosed with multiple metastatic melanoma lesions in his brain. One big tumor appears on a CT scan in the frontal lobe and a MRI shows multiple tumors. They nearly always come as many, the doctor tells us. They know from the pigment deposited in the tumor that it began with the melanoma pigment in his skin. It is my father's skin's response to the struggle of belonging in this land.

I watch the shape of the spot change in response to "Solar-eze," a cream that is also used to treat sunburn for the tens of thousands of white Europeans who still get burned each day. "Do not use over more than a third of your body" the instructions say. I remember sunburn from days at the beach as a child, peeling the skin that came off in thin transparent layers. At times I feel terror about the sun spot, the terror of mortality. Other times I feel it differently. I come to know and love it as a part of me. It is a deeply embodied thing about me and my body in this land. It is the agitation and fear of not belonging, but at the same time it is also the mark of my belonging. It is the shape of my mortality, of the transience of life, an awareness that intensifies the exquisite quality of love that I feel for this landscape.

White II

Leaving, torn apart,
for maybe it's the last time
I'll see the man
that was my Father.

In gentle rocking of the train
I feel self fall
fragment
into the passing scene
of rugged bush and water
of little shacks along the edge
that straddle bush and bay.

I wonder how to live
and why
in that lost and lonely place
when at one house
I see white sheets
pegged billowing in the wind.

It takes me back to time and place
the shack where I gave birth
there blood marked sheets
washed white again
are pegged out on the line
and rows of nappies everyday
blow white in wind and sun.

Leaving Moree the road to Collarenabri is long and straight, lined with spiky gray grass like dead men's whiskers. Even the trees blow dry papery leaves in the winds of drought. Sometimes only silver gray trunks are left standing with empty arms outstretched. Just before Collarenabri we follow a National Parks sign off the main road to find the "Collymongle Scarred Trees." We come to a cage made of heavy metal grid with a metal roof overhead standing in a bare open paddock. A chill wind flurries the dust, the kind of wind that blows across the desert when someone dies. Inside the metal cage there is a stand of nine scarred trees, head and limbs amputated at top and bottom leaving only the stump of branches and trunk. Each tree stump is fixed to a square concrete block inside the metal cage. Circling around the cage it is possible to make out the symbols on the trunks that were once scars on the skin of living trees. These are the marks carved by the Old People, diamond patterns, circles, and curved lines. A sign invites me to photograph the trees but when I place my camera lens inside the squares of metal mesh the camera stops working and never works again. Later when I arrive in Brewarrina, a Ngemba man tells me the spirits of the Old People can never rest while the trees are in the cage.

The nine Aboriginal carved trees in the display come from a traditional initiation ground near Collarenebri.[3] The trees were cut down and moved to Collymongle Station about 60 years ago and placed in the garden of the homestead. The initiation ground is described in detail on the sign. Two circles were linked by a path decorated with designs made from clay and grass and lined with the carved trees. Coolabah, boonery, and belah trees were carved, but the greatest numbers of these were coolabah trees. The curved path was 300 meters long and there were originally 80 carved trees standing along its length. The last time the ground was used for initiations was 1890, and it had been used for tens of thousands of years. A sign with a drawing of the original location of the carved trees evokes the once majestic ceremonial place at the junction of three rivers with its portals of living trees carved with the sacred symbols.

The trees of this country have a remarkable life force drawn from the artesian water in the rock far below. Some of their leaves flicker and sparkle refracting the sun's bright light, others are coated with misty blue-gray against the drying heat. As well as the coolabah, boonery, and belah, there are the western rosewood, the leopard tree, the warrior tree, and the silver-leafed desert ironbark, gidgee, and mulga. Growing all around the trees in their shelter are lots of smaller bushes. In drier ground patches of ancient gidgee and mulga grow, gnarled and dwarfed by their struggle. The ground under them is bare red earth, littered with dry timber. These dead branches seem to have lain there for æons, dry as bone and formed into strange twisted skeletal shapes, the desert life of a Dali painting. The leopard trees are all cut off at head height to feed cattle in these times of drought.

The trees of the initiation ground, the coolabah, boonery, and belah, have names that both hide and reveal their everyday story of place. Only the coolabah takes its name from the Aboriginal language of this country, the Yuwaaliyay word *gulabaa*. It is a typical eucalyptus tree with a silvery mist of eucalyptus oil coating the surface of its blue-gray leaves. Its spreading branches offer much needed shade where "once a jolly swagman/camped by a billabong/under the shade of the coolabah tree." The flowers of the coolabah burst forth from tightly capped buds to become the frothy silken skirts of May Gibbs's gumnut babies. Fully open they reveal the tiny globes of golden pollen on threadlike stamen that brush against native bees attracted to their sweet scent. Once fertilized a shower of tiny hard seeds forms in the tough, woody gumnut, waiting to be spread on the dark gray soils of the flood plain. The coolabah tree grows extensively on these flood plains even without obvious signs of water, but the seeds will only germinate in soil that has been newly flooded. The new seedling needs water to grow, and once grown, each seed becomes a tree world.

The belah tree reaches deep down to the subartesian waters. They drink so deeply of this water that they filter the salt, and if they are cut down the water drawn up by the bores is too salty. Tree and water are one. A typical casuarina, it has no leaves, only long wiry gray-green branchlets with minute fringes of vestigial leaves. There can be no soft places to lose their hard won moisture. Stands of old growth belah trees are very rare because farmers regard it as a weed. The trees in the old growth stands may be over 200 years old, as old as white settlement in this country. Two hundred years is ten generations of people, a story that is longer than living memory. If they are left undisturbed, these old stands of belah trees form mixed woodlands with poplar box and clumps of small bushes underneath. The layered structure of these old growth communities makes a place where lizards, birds, and small animals find shelter. The tiny yellow bellied sheath-tail bat lives in the hollows that only form in these old trees. The white throated tree creeper, red winged parrot, and red-backed fairy wren make their nests there. Trees make worlds.

I eventually find the belah tree buried within lists of Latin names of trees recommended for planting to save endangered birds and animals of the dry country. The belah tree is among a variety of desert trees, including western rosewood, inland rosewood, bullock bush, cattle bush, jiggo, boonery, boneree, bush minga, applebush, and red heart. It grows on the dry red soil ridges that run across the black soil flood plains. The new growth of the boonery tree is said to be dangerously soft, but it soon becomes tough and resilient. It sheds its twisted gray-bark branches in times of drought to lie beside parched carcasses of dead sheep who have succumbed to its toxic leaves. I search for the boonery tree but it now seems to exist only in its song.

It is estimated that six billion trees, 60% of the pre-European tree population, have been cleared from these flood plains since white settlement, primarily for agriculture. Dead trees stand in this landscape like skeletons, the bones of this place, bleached silver like the images that I carry with me from this trip, parched, dry, skeletal, waiting.

By 1944, when the site was recorded by settlers, the initiation ceremonies were long gone from the place of the meeting of the rivers. There were no traces of the figures formed on the ground, the raised earth walls, or the designs made of clay and grass, but 70 carved trees still remained. Today only two living and one dead carved tree stand at the initiation ground. The others were taken away to museums—the National Museum of Victoria, the Museum of Adelaide, the British Museum. The rest were likely souvenired by private collectors. Like the bones of the ancestors, these once living trees that were part of a living culture, were lifted out of their place and removed far from where they belong.

Driving on, we stop to picnic on the banks of the drought-starved Barwon River. The river is a green sluggish trail deep below the marks on the bank of the normal river height. Beside the Barwon, just outside Walgett we stop at a picnic table and nearby notice two more huge metal grid cages, again with amputated trunks of massive trees inside. The grid walls are bolted onto concrete slabs and have a roof over the top. Inside, lying on their side this time, half a dozen tree trunks in each one. All are scarred trees. Some have small scars where a slab of wood has been cut for a coolamon to carry water or a baby, and others have long elliptical shapes where the tree has been cut to make a canoe to travel the waterways.

Each of the hollowed out shapes has the edges rolled in toward the scar where the tree has healed its skin to keep growing. I imagine the hands that cut the shape and honed the wood with a stone implement, the arm that carried the baby next to the breast, the body that carried the canoe that rippled along the smooth watery surface of the river. What does it mean, I wonder, to lock these scarred trees into a wire prison? Why are they here beside the river, who put them there, and who decided that this is where they belong? Do they think someone is going to damage them? Most of the shops and office buildings have bars on the windows. Some are even housed inside cages like the scarred trees. What is the effect on local Aboriginal cultural meanings for this desolate and sad river?

White III

My father once told me
about ashes someone asked
to send to precious family
far away.
He, always saving money,
saving time,
put half the ashes from the jar
into the bin
the other half sent on.

My father now
with no more time to save
white skin withered on bone
becomes again the child he once was
and says,
"I wake not knowing
where I am
I wake not knowing who."

The Daughter says
don't worry
we'll tell you who you are
that ashes will become
we'll tell you line of blood and bone
father daughter son.
He clutches daughter's hand and cries,
then puts the music on,
and wants to dance
for life and love
and happiness soon gone.

My friend and I are now circling the perimeters of the properties that surround the Narran Lake in the towns of Walgett, Lightning Ridge, and Brewarrina. We stay overnight in a motel in the opal mining town of Lightning Ridge, a moonscape of white mullock heaps, a place so hot that many people live underground. Tourist brochures tell us that opal is the national gemstone of Australia, where 97% of the world's opal is produced. It is harvested specifically from these desert areas and Lightning Ridge has the largest known deposits of the precious black opal in the world. Water traveling deep in the earth carries dissolved silica. As it seeps through beds of sand and grit the silica particles gather in cracks and fissures of rock. When the water evaporates, the silica particles are joined together to form opal. When brought into the sun, light diffracted through the stone produces the colors of the opal, from reds to orange, yellow, green, blue, magenta, rose, pink, slate, and olive to black. Of all of these colors, the black opal with its fire of reds and blues is the most rare and the most beautiful.

Lightning Ridge is a place of story. People come from all over the world to search for opals. The name is said to have originated in the 1870s when some passers-by found the bodies of a farmer, his dog, and 600 sheep, all struck by lightning. In 2001 the town had an official population of 1,826 but there are many uncounted people who come there to lose their identity and make their fortune scratching over the white mullock heaps, or if they get lucky, excavating their own mine.

The newsagent has papers in Chinese, Greek, and Arabic, and many other languages. Houses are made from the excavated earth, recycled bottles, left over tin, or dug into deep caverns underground where the opals were once sought. Just out of the town the public artesian baths are a bore tank in a paddock where we lie and watch the light fade and the stars of the Southern Cross appear in the night sky.

We are directed to the Narran Lakes at the Narran Lakes Nature Reserve. I am still looking for *the* Narran Lake and wonder if there is one lake or many. After driving 70 kilometers out of Lightning Ridge on corrugated dirt roads we come to a rusty metal gate with tie wire and a National Parks sign that says no camping. Inside the gate it feels like a different place. It is quiet and still with wheel tracks in soft deep red sand that wind through bare red earth and dwarf forests of mulga, gidgee bush, native cypress, and the occasional tall gum tree. There is lots of dead and fallen timber. The road becomes rocky and the car bottoms out and I inch along winding from side to side to avoid the rocks. After what seems like an eternity, but is only a few kilometers, we arrive at a wide open space with milky tea colored water in small lagoons amidst low bright green succulents and daisies. The bare earth around the lakes is pale pink with craters and lunettes. Beyond the large open area is another smaller lake with water, and beyond that another and another, shining like pearls on a string. Each lake is surrounded by coolabah trees with sparkling leaves that dance in the sun.

As we step out of the car a small white stone tool catches the light on its quartz surfaces, perfectly fashioned with two worked edges and a flat base. I leave it there in its place sparkling in the bright light. The bare pink ground is littered with these shaped stone tools as we walk toward a rise past the remains of an abandoned fence and stockyard. A chill wind is blowing. The rise is not the midden we are looking for but the wall of a small man-made dam. We walk further to the second little lake and disturb a flock of galahs that wheel screeching across the late afternoon sky, pink breasts glowing. Late light now, we start to drive out again, navigating huge gaping holes in the fading light. Alarmed, realize it is too late to leave. No choice but to find a place to pull off the road and camp for the night.

We camp a little way off the road near a small clump of low mulga trees. Bare earth scattered with spiky twisted shapes of dead mulga wood about 50 meters off the road and barely screened by bushes. It feels like the end of the world, so remote, such a depth of silence. It is midwinter and still early, but the last light is almost gone as we hastily erect the tent, make a small fire, and eat some food. Crawl into sleeping bags as pointer stars and then the Southern Cross appear in a vast night sky and the desert cold comes up from the ground.

I sleep on and off on a hard thin sleeping mat and half asleep, half dreaming, I wake with a start. The dream-state is strange: we are camping here in this place but it is a bigger camp and during the night some unexpected visitors arrive. Two young Aboriginal children come into our tent in a friendly way and help themselves to some of our food, which is in another tent behind us. They give some of the food to their parents who are in a big sort of camping station wagon. Then a big mob of Aboriginal people join us at the camp beside the water, and there is talking and laughing, much happiness at being together in this place. I feel like I am part of all this in some present-distant time.

Then I am abruptly fully awake, "Did you hear those gun shots?" Lie frozen and listen as several more gun shots sound in the silent night air. I can see on mobile phone it's 1.30 a.m. and register that there's no coverage. Stay absolutely still, afraid that whoever is firing the shots will find us. A heavy vehicle drives slowly toward the camp on the road. Terrified now, wait to hear if it goes out the gate beyond our camp. It drives past and then turns and comes back again. Panic sets in. Wake in fright. Rape, murder in the bush, what to do—run, lie quiet, drive? Heart pounding, lie rigid as silence settles, this time an eerie silence, filled with fear. Struggling to still the terror, it is only by reentering the space of my dream-state where I feel safe among a group of Aboriginal people living their lives by the lake that I can sleep again.

Just before dawn the truck goes past again but this time the sound disappears into the distance. They seem to have gone out the gate and kept going. They have obviously been here all night. At first light we get up to plan a way out of our night of terror. We discover we each have the same paranoid fear that they have locked the gate to keep us in. We are curious about how to read these strange events. We track the marks of their truck back and forth across the wide open space of green succulents and daisies, and the drops of blood trailing behind the tyre marks. Who were they and why were they here in this forbidden place? Why were they shooting? Why did they come back? We cannot read the local in this place. It feels as if we are a million miles from nowhere but there are obviously people around here who may well be aware of our presence. Then there is the deeper underlying bedrock fear that as white people we shouldn't be here in this country at all.

We make a fire and boil a billy of tea in the early morning sun beside the little lake and make our peace with that place before we leave for Walgett, the closest place to the "real" Narran Lake. When I had asked Chrissiejoy before our trip how to see the lake near Walgett she laughed and said, "You silly whitefellas, of course you can't see the lake, it's on private property, one property owns half, and the other, where I grew up, owns the other half." When I questioned her further she said, "There is no water in the lake anyway, the whitefellas take all the water out of the river. Whether there is water in the Narran River depends on how much water comes down from Queensland. All dammed up on Cubby Station to feed the cotton." Once in Walgett I decide to go to the Tourist Information Centre to ask if they can help me to find the Narran Lake. They are friendly and helpful and after a few phone calls the woman has permission for us to visit one of the properties that now encloses the lake.

We set off for the property, 10 kilometers on the road to Goodooga, then 30 odd kilometers of dirt on the Narran Lake Road. The relatively small cattle property of 22,000 acres is a few further kilometers off the road with a modest weatherboard house where we sit on the front veranda with three generations of family, grandmother, son, and baby. They talk a lot about the drought, about "the Aboriginal problem," about the grandkids. They show us photos of the place with not a blade of anything growing on the bare pink earth. They sold all the cattle in the drought and are buying them back now because of recent rains but, they tell us, people are saying the drought is not over yet.

The lake is mostly an interesting absence in this conversation. I wonder if this is because it is dry, or because it is contentious and they don't know us, or maybe it is just a taken-for-granted part of their everyday farming life. The son tells us that the lake has been dry for three years. He says it is huge, a hundred kilometers to drive around it when it is full. He becomes animated briefly when recalling the lake with water in it, "It's unreal" he says, "because of all the migratory birds, the magpie geese come there, and the strawberry ibis, they all breed there." And he talks about the snakes, "The lake is full of snakes, especially King Browns, but at the moment, if you see any, they'll be hibernating." The grandmother says "They won't let us crop the lake, only on a receding flood."

It is hard to get away but we have been sitting and talking for an hour and we are anxious to see the lake before it gets dark. They tell us how to navigate ourselves through numerous gates and paddocks with a clear picture in their heads of the way to go but I have no idea how I will find the way in the big white university car. I wonder why they don't come with us, why they trust us to find our way around their place. I nervously drive the big white car alongside dams on narrow muddy tracks gouged with wheel ruts from recent rains. We finally arrive at a gate that opens onto the place where we have been directed to go to see the lake. Still looking, we can't decide which way to go because all we can see is a sea of lush green. Along its edges there appear to be levee channels or maybe a road that runs back along the fence toward the house, and in the other direction the wheel tracks lead into the never-ending green. It is impossible to get much further because the road is so deeply buried in the green. We drive just a little in each direction but there is nothing more to see—just green stretching from horizon to horizon.

Driving back along the road at dusk we float in a luminous dome of light that fades from clear bright blue to palest blue-green flushed with apricot along the western horizon. The road is straight and the landscape flat in every direction but the horizon is so wide and clear that it is possible to discern the round curve of the earth's surface.

So open, so still, and so straight, the road seems to stretch forever into the fading light. We arrive at Bokhara Plains Hutz, the local farmstay homestead, just as the last light goes from the sky. It is the only place to stay around here so government employees, farm workers, and visitors are all housed in a farm hut and shearing quarters, a few hundred meters from the house. Everyone is invited to eat at the homestead. The walk between house and shearing quarters is filled with the blackest night sky, no lights out here. On the way to dinner the evening star and the Southern Cross appear bright in the sky above us. On the way back to the shearing quarters we are suspended in the silver star-spun orb of the revolving night sky.

In that moment of standing in country I am aware of the arc of movement of silver stars across black night sky formed by the turning of the earth. I trace a line of thought and story from the gathering images of country beginning with that first writing from touch of skin on skin, the space between self and other, self and world. In finger on skin it is always the movement, the tracing that one senses, that dislodges the images that can be articulated into form. In that movement of flesh becoming word, the images take shape as black marks that now lie across the white sheet.

In the beginning of the world, Immiboagurramilbun says, there is always Mulgury. "Every tracing, every rock, tree, plant, landform, the water, fish, reptile, bird, animal is Mulgury and the pattern, shape and form of Mulgury is life, and all is a continuing tracing of Mulgury." In Gumbaynggirr country we traced the movement of feet in walking trails where the lines of movement connect one special place to another. The line of a foot walking across Gumbaynggirr country is the very songline, what is so exalted in Western translation. Songlines are simply the cultural practice of walking through Country following the trails. The longer the trail, the more one needs a map to guide one's way. In Gumbaynggirr country the stars are the guide, represented in the placement of stones on the high peaks, stones that follow the diamond constellation of the stars of the Southern Cross. The pattern of stars of the Southern Cross is also Birrugan, the creation hero whose actions created the walking trails, the line of story and of song. In the drylands these are trails of water places.

White IV

Tracing a line
of finger on skin
of foot in country
of stars in black night sky
a line of thought
of space
on fine white sheet,
of crescent moon shaped dip in hill,
the changing space of light
as sky revolves from day to night
and night to day
in silver turning of the world.

In the morning we stand at the horse yard beside three big stock horses as we take our leave. I ask Kathy, who runs the homestay, if it is the Bokhara River over the back and she says, "Yes, it is the Bokhara River, but I don't know why they call it a river, it's just a creek really." Later I look on the map and the Bokhara rises in Queensland and travels all the way down to Brewarrina where it joins up with the Namoi and Barwon Rivers to become the Darling. The Bokhara Plains, of the property name, are the black soil plains of the Bokhara River, watered by the floods that bring the fertile black soil to their land. Around the river the black soil is dried into a craze of deep cracks in the place where water once traveled. I try to engage Kathy in conversation about the Narran Lake. I tell her about our visit to the property, that all we could see was lush green so it was hard to find the edges of the lake, to even know what we were looking at. She says she thinks it is wheat, that they crop the lake, but when she turns to her husband he is even more cautious, not giving anything away to strangers. Kathy, however, knows local Ngemba man Bradley Steadman who lives in Brewarrina, so she organizes us to meet with him and talk to him about the Narran Lake.

Driving into Brewarrina on the Kamilaroi Highway we pass a faded sign that says "Welcome to Brewarrina" across the top, and below it is a picture of a lake with a swan, an ibis, and a goose. Underneath the picture it says: "Narran Lake. This lake is the largest freshwater lake in NSW. It has the largest ibis rookery in the world and is home for all forms of bird life."

The sign stands on bare red earth scattered with low succulents beside a long straight stretch of highway and a flat blue horizon. The lake that is nowhere to be found. Every few hundred meters along the road there is yet another sign that asks visitors to spend $20 in Brewarrina to save the town.

We meet Brad Steadman in the neatly mown front yard of a small fibro house.[4] He directs us to the fish traps on the river at the end of the main street of town. We stand on a high bank looking down on a wide expanse of shallow water that flows over a weir and disappears around a bend in the other direction. Curved patterns of rocks make ripples of silver light and creamy bubbles of froth, on the milky surface of the water. Brad arrives on his pushbike. "When I was a kid living on the river," he says, "you could hear the water running over the rocks and you could tell whether the river was rising or falling by the sound." The curved patterns of rocks are fish traps built by the Old People, "Three layers across the width of the river. Each has an opening that they used to close with rocks to catch the fish as they swam up the river."

In the time of the dreaming, he tells us, the river dried up during a big drought and there was nothing to eat. The creator cast his net over the river and made the patterns of the rocks. He showed the old men of the Ngemba people how to make the rain by dancing and singing. Days of rain followed and the river flooded, bringing thousands of fish. The old men rushed to block the entry of the stone traps, herding the fish into the pens. The creator told them that although the Ngemba people were the custodians of the fishery, the fish traps were to be shared with other tribes of the area, "the Morowari, Paarkinji, Weilwan, Barabinja, Ualarai, and Kamilaroi."[5] Each group had a different yard that they could take their fish from so there was no problem with using and sharing the fish.

Brad says his people have been fishing here for at least 40,000 years. Each of the rocks has a name and there is a story about the giant fish Ngunnhu that lives in the waterhole above the weir. This was in the times when there was no weir and no river, only a deep waterhole where Ngunnhu lived. The creator caught the giant fish and he thrashed around breaking the banks of the waterhole so the water trickled out, forming the Darling River that flows all the way down past the bend to meet the Murray River. The water here used to be so clear you could see the duckweed with the fish swimming in and out, it was not silted all the time like it is today. You used to be able to see your hand under the water, now you can't even see your fingers. In the old days when the clear water became milky the people knew that it was time for the fish to come up the river. Even today, Brad says, people still use the fish traps and catch fish in them using fishing lines or tree guards. *Tree guardin'* they call it.

Brad's great grandmother was born on the banks of the river, back toward Walgett, and was brought in to Brewarrina to live on the Mission. She could remember the paddle steamers coming up the Darling River to Brewarrina to pick up the wool in the old days. Lots of people were trucked in from country to the north and west to Brewarrina, all mixed in together and put on the Mission—Paakantji, Muruwari, Yuwaalaraay and his own people the Ngemba—all river people. Even people from the desert lands of South Australia, the Arabana, were brought in to the Brewarrina Mission.

We talk a lot about this place and their stories of the river. He makes a circle with his finger and thumb on one hand to show how local knowledge has become contracted. Then he holds both arms outstretched and open as if to embrace all of his country, "We need to expand our knowledge, to build it up again."

"As a visitor to this country," Brad says, "you can go anywhere and see a beautiful place but you will not know its story." I tell him I am interested in hearing its stories and ask about the Narran Lake. He explains that he cannot speak for the Narran Lake, there are old people in Walgett who can take me out there and who know its stories. They speak a different language and they know different stories. They also know stories of the fish traps but they cannot speak for the fish traps. He says there is a footprint of the creator in the rock at the edge of the river next to the fish traps that links them to the prints of the creator and his dog where they sat down to rest at the Narran Lake.

Brad leads us down closer to the water's edge beside the dancing, sparkling light of the river and shows us its connection to the Narran Lake. He points out the footprint of the creator in a big flat rock beside the rocky net pattern of fish traps. Part of the foot is silted over but several giant toes, the arch and ball of a giant foot are plainly visible. "That footprint," he says, "is a sentence in the Aboriginal story."

Map 3: Mud Map of Country

3
THINKING THROUGH COUNTRY[1]

I continue my search for the Narran Lake by playing Chrissiejoy's DVD and listening to the rhythm of her voice, low pitched and slow. I look over and over again at the paintings that she has made to help articulate a methodology of the Narran Lake. Although these paintings and words are the basis of thinking through Country, I have not dwelled in this place with deep, close attention before. I begin with the mauve circle outlined in red containing the yellow shape of Noongahburrah country held within the lines of the rivers. My eye is drawn along the fine black lines of water to the thickening black of the Narran Lake. This is where place becomes Country for me and I want to understand the process and its meanings.

"A Mud Map of Country" (Conceptual Framework)

Starting in the centre top of the painting this jigsaw piece is viewed as a mud map of the Noongahburrah country. The black lines are the rivers within, and marking the boundaries of this country, and the black orb in the centre represents the Narran Lake, where I was raised, and which has always been the most significant and sacred site for Noongahburrah, Murriburrah, Ngunnaburrah, and all the other peoples of the nation that spoke the U'Alayi language as well as several other nations of Aboriginal people within bordering countries. (Immiboagurramilbun)[2]

Immiboagurramilbun learned U'Alayi[3] culture from her Noongah-burrah[4] grandfather and uncles as she grew up by the Narran Lake. Her grandmother, who lived there with them, was Erinbinjori (people of the Crocodile) from far north Queensland, and her father was a white station owner. Immiboagurramilbun through kinship has authority to speak to all of these knowledge traditions. She came to me as a doctoral student and struggled with her desire to conform to academic language and knowledge structures. Liberated by my encouragement, over a period of several years Chrissiejoy developed a radical alternative methodology for her research. Although researching the development of a training package in conflict resolution and now living in Sydney, Chrissiejoy realized that in order to make any knowledge claims at all she had to think through Country, the specific country of the Narran Lake. She produced a DVD as the basis of the presentation of her methodology in the doctoral program, *Calling up Blackfella Knowing through Whitefella Magic*. It is this DVD that we later modified to inform the methodology for our collaborative research. We called it *Thinking through Country*, an articulation of the unremarkable fabric of everyday life. It is the space of Chrissiejoy's images and words that I enter in writing this chapter.

Taking up Chrissiejoy's invitation to think through Country connects me back to that primal scene of doing ceremony with women in the desert as a young wife and mother. I had moved there with my husband's appointment as a teacher and the old women found me with access to a four-wheel drive. For them, all women with children knew ceremony. How many times have I returned to that scene? There were no words through which to understand, only sound, music, body design, and dancing—in Country. I have written over and over again about this memory which precipitated a life's work, but the words cannot carry the depth or the meaning of the experience. Suspended in the liminal, the images from that time and place wait in my body until they resonate with thinking through Country.

I recall my body memory of the desert, the desert's nmesic scar in me. I remember being rubbed all over breasts and shoulders and belly with kangaroo fat, the patting of my pregnant belly, no words. The touch of careful finger tips making designs on my white skin in red, yellow, and white ochres as the sound of singing grows louder and then fades away. I can feel the vibration in my body from the deep visceral chanting, the resonant click of clapsticks, and the thud of feet on bare earth. Each of these vibrations comes from the same energy field, up through the soles of my feet on the ground to a particular space in my heart center, a center of energy in my body. Feet to body through deep red earth.

The designs are always the same—parallel curved lines on shoulders and breast—each line a different color, each with a song. Designs made of coarse powdery ochres held on skin coated with kangaroo fat. What I remember now is the slightly gritty feel of ochre and fat against my clothes when I return from the desert to my usual place inside a house on a government settlement cooking dinner for my husband and children. A feeling of incredulity, did that really happen? Of two worlds that cannot know each other, a profound disjuncture.

After listening and dwelling in Chrissiejoy's voice talking Country, I wake in the night thinking I have no country. While Chrissiejoy assembles her identities in her suburban home in western Sydney, and presents them in a seminar room at the University of New England on the northern tablelands of New South Wales, the Narran Lake remains the center of her story. She belongs to this country, the center of her being and her understanding of the world. How can I learn to think through Country if I have no country?

Where is my country?
Is it Sydney, the suburban bush where I grew up?
Is it Scotland, the place my four
    grandparents always called home?
Is it the desert, that first inarticulate place of
    belonging in this Australian landscape?
Is it Armidale where I was transformed
    through its Aboriginal stories?
Is it that place on the blue shores of Sydney
    Harbour where I imagine my Old People are?

Is it the green grass and forests of Gippsland,
   the place of this writing?

Or is it my body
in any place?
and what is the body,
is it only the body-in-connection-with
all places,
and the practice of a body-in-place
is a practice of Country?

Feet. I massage feet. I listen, the torn foot, the patching of the torn foot, the torn finger the knife the stitching. The feel of the foot as a map of country. What is unrepresentable is the space in between. The abyss.

You and me and country. We are sitting on two chairs in front of the kitchen fire in your house with your feet on my legs on a towel because of the oil. I massage your feet with comfrey ointment that your Aunty has made (I could write a whole novel about this one moment). I feel the comfrey ointment, feel into its pale green color, a slight fragrance of lavender, its quality of touch, not like oil, not so light and slippery, but more like the beeswax ointment with lavender that I have for sleeping beside my bed. To massage with it is better than oil because it has a slight resistance to the touch. Something suspended, more living, it enables more feel of skin. I place a thumbful of this ointment that your Aunty has made to help your healing on the ball of your foot and begin to spread the ointment over all of your foot. Your feet are long and slender, the toes are long, and like all toes, so beautifully formed.

The skin is dry and a little loose as I move my fingers over skin, muscle, and bone, feeling the shapes of foot, becoming-foot. I have no thoughts, no plan, no massage technique, I am quite lacking in either knowledge or confidence, it is just something I am doing, absorbed in the moment of foot. My hand is feeling into this foot, not seeing, but feeling. On this foot I feel difference. While I feel, you tell me the story. The story is congruent with the feel of your foot. The voice telling the story is part of becoming foot, I am aware that I do not take in the details of this story, except to know that the foot has been ripped apart by the impact of the accident. I hear the telling of the shoe, that you took the shoe off in the helicopter on the way to hospital but it was not until days later that they operated on the foot. "This foot has lost its muscle definition" you say, "it feels different, strange."

I know this feeling because I can feel it in my finger where my finger was cut with my very sharp carbon steel butcher's knife and the nerves were severed. In this finger I feel the slight tingly unpleasant sensation of no feeling, the ridgy scar on that finger where the nerves were severed. That one finger does not work so well and makes me feel clumsy in small precise movements, like opening door locks. I know this feeling. I feel it on the sole of your foot. I can feel the ridgy-ness where there is a line of repair where two pieces of skin have been joined together again but they don't quite mesh. Some of this we talk, some is just going through my head but where I am really is in this foot, hand and foot together becoming one, my hand feeling your foot through my own long-ago story of the knife, a story of a lifetime, and your foot a more recent not-yet-healed story of today. Mapping the territory of the body through the scars of bodies and stories, mapping what I can know of the other.

"Me, Myself and I" (Ontology)

At the beginning all was Mulgury[5] Only creative power and intent. Through the intent and power of our Creator, Mulgury reproduces into form to carve the beings and shapes of the world where the water meets the sky and earth sings the world to life. The pattern of life is Mulgury and Mulgury is traced in the Niddrie [the framework of the ancient laws within Niddeerie] of Mudri [person]. Every tracing, every rock, tree, plant, landform, the water, fish, reptile, bird, animal and Mudri is in the sacred relationship, through Niddeerie.[6] The pattern, shape and form of Mulgury is life, and all is a continuing tracing of Mulgury. (Ticalarn-abrewillaring, 1961; translated by Immiboagurramilbun, 2005)[7]

I dwell in the idea of Mulgury from a place of unknowing and hope that through this dwelling and writing I will come to know. Immiboagurramilbun begins with swan. In the image that represents her ontology she paints four black swans. The first two swans are for her mother, and the second two represent the collective of water people, the Noongahburrah, her grandfather's people. In her culture, one swan on its own is a warning of bad omens. The swans are Mulgury, signaling their collective meaning as mythical creatures of the Niddeerie, as well as representing an individual's connection to a particular creature and its place. Immiboagurramilbun's mother is swan, Noongahburrah people collectively are swan. Swan belongs to the time and place of the creation of the land and people of Terewah, the home of the black swan, in the past, the present, and the future. Those who carry that identity are both swan and place. Country, swan, and person are together an ontological reality.

Immiboagurramilbun says that as an Aboriginal person you are given a Mulgury at birth and it comes with responsibility for that animal or plant and is part of you and you of it. Part of that obligation is to learn all about your Mulgury and everything that is connected to it. If your Mulgury was the kangaroo, you would learn that you are related to the trees, the insects, the birds, the grass, the wind, the rain, and all the things which occur and surround a kangaroo's life. You would spend years observing and learning about the life of your Mulgury—what it needs to survive and how it assists in the survival of other species. Most importantly, you would learn how all those things connect to yourself—how they all become your brothers and sisters, part of your family, and about the responsibility that goes with it.

Dwelling in the idea of Mulgury,[8] I recall the story of the dry grass blowing against the fence.

> I've seen 'em too go and get that—
> you might see a lot of grass up against
> a tree or a fence
> very soft grass
> and they'd go and get that
> and it'd blow like the wind
> they'd go and get this
> and they'd stuff it into bags
> and they'd make bed ticks out of them
> they used this a lot, dry grass

that catches up on the netting fences
they used that as a bed tick
it was just as soft as a bed to sleep on
it's very warm in winter
because it warms up and keeps the heat
that is what a lot of them done
this is about what I know.

(BILL LOVELOCK)[9]

I responded to the arrangement of these lines on a page with a recognition of presence and absence, of the sensory presence of the body
in this story, and my own body's absence in the storied landscapes of
this place. It seemed a matter of a failure to express my bodily presence in written language that simultaneously reproduced an absenting
of my body-in-place. Now, in dwelling in the idea of Mulgury, I have
a body memory of the backstory that could not be told at the time. My
family and I left the desert and drove thousands of kilometers across
Australia looking for a new home. We finally arrived at a rudimen-
tary share farmer's cottage in a soldiers' settlement orchard area 30
kilometers out of Armidale. My memory of the white fibro cottage,
with its matching gables and faded blue corrugated iron roof, still fills
me with a sense of homecoming. Six dollars a week, it was all that we
could afford, having left the desert and paid work—a place to land,
to have a new baby. Building beds out of old cast-off wardrobes, collecting fruit-fall from the orchard next door, mushrooms from the hill
behind, trapping rabbits to cook, and gathering pine cones to burn for
warmth, for cooking, and for hot water.

Body/place memories are particular—the apple hanging in the
tree, the apple in the garden. The roundness of it, the sight of its moon
roundness in the half-light of dusk hanging in its part hidden place
beneath the tree. Not in the moonlight but the half-light of dusk, that
time when day crosses over into night and apple steals from the last
light of day—the round belly of my pregnancy with my third baby,
the baby who was so loved. Finding that farmhouse, the place with
all the qualities of home—the double gable, timber walls, built lightly
on the land, cleared paddocks marked by thickened rows of pine trees
planted to make parcels of land that were given to soldier settlers. The

orchards that they planted, now almost derelict, not picked, are left for us, for me with my round belly.

The apples signify the grace card of that space, they stand for it all, the daily lighting of the fire, the chip heater, the pine cones that come from that very marking out of the soldier settler divisions, the peaches, but most of all the apples. They hang heavy on the trees, their fleshy weight bending the branches when the trees start to lose their leaves. They have lost all their leaves when the last apples still hang there. We pick only enough to eat each day. Why would you pick more when they will wait there for the picking? As the season grows, the days shorten, and the cold comes, the frost touches the apples, their skin shows the blush of the cold touch of winter. The rose blush appears, not as a single splash of color but as masses of tiny rose colored stars sprinkled over green. The green apples turn to gold until they glow golden lanterns on bare dark twigs. These last precious apples, because they will soon all be gone, are so unbelievably sweet. I know by the change of color, the appearance of the blush, the golden glow beyond green, their weight on the tree, the loss of leaves, and look of bare branches just one or two apples left on their outline, tree against sky, twisted twigs of branches with the miracle of golden orbs, the last fruits of autumn, that it will all soon be gone for another cycle of seasons.

In the misty rains of autumn we find circles of white mushrooms in the damp grass. We look underneath the white domes to find the perfect pink-fawn pleats and white collar around the stem. We know then they are good ones to eat. On the way back from the mushroom hill we walk into thickets of pine trees planted in deep rows that divide the square paddocks from each other. Underneath, on a soft bed of pine needles, are scatters of pine cones—the old ones are too rotten for burning, the new are too green. The ones we collect are somewhere in between, hard and partly open with perfectly formed ledges, like shingles on a roof protecting the seed inside. These ones, with some dry pine needles, are just right to light the old Metters stove for cooking apples, mushrooms, and rabbit.

In the cold times of winter we snare rabbits in steel traps, venturing out into the hard white frost of dawn to find them. Breath steams in morning air, face and fingers tingle with cold. We kill the rabbits quickly to stop their pain and peel the furred skin inside out like peeling off rubber gloves. The inside of the skin is still warm and pliable, a map of veins laced with pink. The skins are stretched inside out to dry over bent wire coat hangers for tanning. They hang in rows on the clothesline across the back yard beside washing frozen stiff in the winter cold. The naked body of the rabbit is slit down the middle of the belly to lift the organs out gently and separate what is cooked from what is discarded. Soft pink inside flesh is cut into chunks at bone joints, knife feeling through gristle, lower limbs, upper limbs, body around rib cage. All is placed in a big stewing pot with carrots, parsnips, potatoes, celery from the garden, and put on to simmer over a fire of pine cones on the old Metters stove. Rabbit stew keeps us alive. Apples, mushrooms, pine needles, and rabbits are the unremarkable fabric of our everyday life. They are my way of being in Country.

"Reading Country" (Epistemology)

> The continuation outside of time is Niddeerie; The Niddeerie is Country and the life that is one with Country; The people from Country are one with all that is made of Country; Our ancestors speak with "us-of-the-Niddeerie," to give and keep the Niddrie; The lore is the strength and privilege of life that is given through the Niddeerie; The freedoms of Country are granted neither by wealth or force but through Niddrie; Our Wise Ones gain their wisdom and knowledge from Niddeerie, power from the Ancestors; And strength from Country, as do all our people. The lore; Niddrie; Country; all living and Spiritual things; Past, present and future; Our lives and those after; all belong in Niddeerie. It is all connected. (Ticalarnabrewillaring, 1960, translated by Immiboagurramilbun, 2005)

How do we come to know? In Immiboagurramilbun's thinking through Country all knowledge is knowledge of Country and all has its origins in the Niddeerie.[10] Niddeerie is the time when all things come into being, so it is connected to the understanding of being through Mulgury. All the forms of life, Mulgury, materialize in the

Niddeerie which embodies past, present, and future. Through Mulgury, Niddeerie can be understood as the coming into being of all the forms of life, and of tracings, mark making, language, and ideas, taking form simultaneously with country. The creation of the world is the same process in which thinking through Country is materialized in Immiboagurramilbun's paintings, or the black marks on a white page, tracings through which I can come to know. The Niddeerie is told in stories.

I imagine Immiboagurramilbun's grandmother living by Terewah, the Narran Lake, teaching her about how the world is made, about the swans and the lake. The Grandmother told her the story of Kurreah who made the lake. The giant lizard swallowed the Creator's two wives when they went to collect yams. Baiame, the Creator, then tracked Kurreah from dried up waterhole to waterhole swallowing the water as he went. When Baiame came to some wet mud he knew Kurreah was there inside that waterhole and he killed the giant lizard to rescue his wives. As he was dying, Kurreah thrashed his giant tail from side to side making the shape of the Narran Lake. In 1960, the date on the translation of the Grandmother's words about the Niddeerie, Immiboagurramilbun was 14 years old, the time of a young woman's initiation into womanhood. What stories can we tell our granddaughters now so that they too can come to know Country?

Stealing time in that precious hour before dawn again, a thief in the night I write a story about plums. Walking along the rail trail[11] find red seedling plums growing among green leaves on a wet leafy plum tree. The plums are small, mottled red and yellow, many ripe ones, skin and seeds scattered on the ground. We try some ripe ones because we forgot our lunch. Further along another tree, this time the plums are a deep maroon when ripe so we eat some more. These ones taste slightly different. Still further a bright yellow one and then finally, a larger deep gold plum, dripping from the tree, so ripe they drop as fingers reach into wet leafy branches to receive golden fruit. Sweet and luscious. On the way back we collect plums from each of the trees until our hats are full. I put them in a bowl in the kitchen to enjoy the bright colors, the reds, yellows, maroons, and golds. Each day the miracle of plum color unfolds. Red plums change from red-tinged-green to bright red to maroon to almost black, the deepest dark maroon I have ever seen. How is it, I wonder, that color is produced and changes so day by day? What does it mean to eat color?

I remember when my children were small making our daily breakfast with plums from a tree in the garden. So I take out the bowl and pick out a large handful of ripe red plums. I cut them carefully one by one, taking the flesh from the stone. Even the inside flesh is red. The plums are quite small so cutting them is slow and time consuming. To cut these small ripe plums the carbon steel knife is honed sharp. I feel the quality of ripe plum flesh with my fingers as I select them by color for ripeness. Only the really ripe ones are fully flavored. To cut them I find the line of the invisible seed. Each plum has the line of a fold that runs lengthwise from the stem to base. The line of the fold tells me just where to place the sharp steel knife to run smoothly through the soft moist flesh and cut it free from the seed.

The fold is the line of the outside world folding inside, where the plum blossom was fertilized by the bee to make a new plum tree. I place the knife along the fold. The knife follows the fold of the plum, the line that contains the traces of its origins, its femaleness. I remember the line that appears on my belly when I am soon to give birth. A dark line that marks the white skin, starting at the knot of umbilical cord, the line of the plum. The line that signals the coming of childbirth that rents one body in two, the flesh that was one leaving the mother to become an other. I remember that moment with each baby, the precise place, time, and body moment of all-time all-place. As I slice through soft sweet flesh I place the seeds in the compost bucket and the round sweet cheeks of plum into my breakfast to eat of the shady rail trail walk.

The next summer we go plum picking with my daughter, big with her second baby Lily. We find seedling plums on roadside trees from the bright yellow or red fruit. Look into tree for color, feel the softness of flesh, and eat a handful from each tree, then pick what we can reach. With three pairs of hands picking we soon have several buckets full, laughing and filling different buckets with different colored plums, telling stories of picking feral food. Back at home, we unload all the plums and begin the work of cutting off the tiny bits of flesh from the seed to make jam and chutney. We talk about the laborious work of cutting out the seed—whether to boil the fruit whole or cut the seeds out first. We make a small amount of red plums into jam by cutting out the seeds, then we make a big pot of red ones with seeds removed, and leave the yellow plums to boil whole and skim the seeds off the top. As we cut the seeds we talk and laugh about our new Gippsland plum baby.

The story of plums grew out of grief. The shock of the skin cancer, how fast it grew on the skin of the face, the white scar. The advice of no more sun on my skin, for ever. At first I was frightened of the sun—wore sunscreen, hat, long sleeves, trousers. The hat restricted my vision, like having a dark cloud over my head. I feel as if my life has changed forever, longing for the feel of air and sun. Walking the rail trail feels safe and healing, shaded by tall gums, the air of trees. The shade is cool and gentle to fair, sun-damaged skin. It is the commons that I inhabit there, the margins that feed me with feral food, wild plums with a life force to heal. Now I have a map of plum places in country and a new baby born into plum stories. The jam is exquisite, the taste of the skin comes out more fully in the cooking and the jam is a much stronger flavor than the raw fruit. It is feral food at its best. Mother, daughter, baby, friend, plums, and country, where the water meets sky and earth sings the world to life.

Country is not place, but nor is it nature or environment. There is no separation of human activity and the natural world; Country includes mining holes in the ground, the grid of cities, built environments, industry, farms, and roads. Country acknowledges these as layers, superinscribed over the shapes of the landscape—hills, valleys, water, rock, and stone. It acknowledges the pain and trauma of destructive forces and actions with grief and emotion. Country never loses the sense that the original creation story is still always there, in the meaning of that particular location, in the shapes of the land, in its ongoing stories told in plums and words.

"Finding and Knowing Place of Self and Others within Country" (Methodology)

> As children we spent much time following the life cycle of the grub, as we did with all other animals, birds, insects and plant life. We would learn when they mated, how the mother prepared for her babies, we watched the young grubs grow and we knew how to know when they reached maturity. You can imagine the depth of knowledge gained from this kind of learning. It not only gave knowledge about the insect itself, but also about everything that is connected to it, the type of conditions most favoured. We learned what happened when floods or drought hit the area, what the grub needed for survival and what other animals and birds fed on the grub itself. In addition, we were shown how it all connected to us. (Immiboagurramilbun)

I am sitting on red dirt in the sparse dry shade of a silver leafed mulga tree with six women. We've been digging for grubs in a little forest of mulga trees. At each tree the women loosen the hard earth with the pointy end of their digging sticks and dig down to the roots. Then with fingers removing the loose earth they trace the line of root where they will find the white grubs. More digging, carefully this time, along the length of the root, which is lifted out and prised open with fine movements of fingers so as not to damage the delicate flesh inside. The grub lies in a bed of fine wood dust within the woody core, made weak by its presence. It is plucked out, skin silky and cool like the silkworms of childhood. Each is placed in a billycan until there is a bundle of wriggling white. Digging sticks, hard wood worn smooth from their labor are now lying beside us and a small fire of gnarled mulga wood burns to coals and ash. The fat white bodies of witchetty grubs are laid into the hot sand beside the fire. Grub body flicks out stiff and straight, crisp skin crackling golden with fat from within its body.

Chrissiejoy says this is a practical methodology, a methodology of practice. I wonder what is my practice of Country here now, in this other place? My first response is a story about lemons. Walking to collect lemons from Jes's place and letting my response in lemons flow through my body in images. They are images of all the lemons in all of their places and all the lemon stories. Each story has a body/place connection in images. Bright gold of lemons on dark green trees in a cold gray Victorian winter.

I remember the first time I saw lemons when walking around Churchill getting to know the place, five years ago now. Streets and streets of same houses, no one outside, too cold, dead, and quiet. But at one house, a white-washed dome shape and a tree dripping with lemons. People don't seem to pick them so they stay on the trees, golden lights in winter gloom. In Jes's garden there's an old Meyer lemon tree, the kind that are dark, rich, gold skinned, and sweet. A prolific tree, when someone invited me to dinner just after I arrived, I took a bag of lemons for a present. They looked at the beautiful lemons in the bag, "Everyone here has too many lemons," they said, "we don't even pick them."

I've started eating lemons in a serious way. Jes and I have decided to practice being "frugarian," to live with less in response to the needs of the planet. I recall Pauliina's question of the people from the villages in the north of Finland (Rautio & Lanas, 2011). Many people have left these small villages and the story is that villages are dying. Pauliina asked the women in the village: "What is a good enough life?" and to write letters to her about "What is beautiful in your everyday life?" One woman wrote:

> I was making zucchini salad in the kitchen. I had taken lettuce and zucchini from my garden. I was just dicing the zucchini as I heard my daughter begin to play the violin in the living room. Suddenly I was all there—present in the moment: I heard the violin, the hum of the washing machine from the laundry room. I felt the moist, soft skin of the zucchini. I saw pearls of water droplets on its green and silvery striped skin. And then I was in the forest again. As if I had returned there through the skin of the zucchini.

Back from Jes's now I have a bowl full of lemons freshly picked from the tree. Not like the weekly shopping when I used to have every sort of fruit whether in season or out, from Woolworth's shelves. I have lemons. Every morning I start the day with the juice of a lemon squeezed in a glass of tepid water. On my breakfast of grated apple and oats, I squeeze another lemon and remember that even though long ago I substituted oranges for lemons in this recipe, it was lemons in the original Bircher muesli. Then in the evening I make juice of carrot, beetroot, celery, and a whole lemon dropped into the juicer. The addition of the rind sharpens the taste. The lemons are all free and they are so of this place, golden lights in winter gray. I think about lemons as a practice of everyday life, a practical way of thinking through Country.

What might a practice of Country look like? I think about the local practices of everyday life from the Gumbaynggirr stories of *Singing the Coast*—building shelters, making do, recycling, and especially stories of "eating place." Yarrawarra people lived on prawns, crabs, and fish from the estuary; turtles, swamp hens, and eels from the swamp; pipis, googumbals, and abalone from the beach and rock pools; mullet, tailor, mackerel, whiting, jewfish, bream, and trevally from the sea; kangaroos, possum, and porcupine from the surrounding bushlands; and turtles, eels, and cobra from the river. In between all of these places people ate native fruits such as lilli pillis, wild cherries, nyum nyums, and pigface as they walked on their tracks through the dunes and coastal heathlands. When they tell stories about eating all of these things they are stories of the local food ecologies of collecting, preparing, cooking, and eating from local places.

In thinking through lemons, I work from the body in images that are held in the body in prelanguage form, like the images that stayed with me from my trip to the Narran Lake. In thinking through Country it is the inseparable connection between body and place, the space of that unarticulated relation that I want to make present. It is a space that I access through my original insight from the story of the grass blowing up against the fence that the body was present in a way that I could not yet realize in my work. It is from that primal sense that there was body/place connection in the words, the grass blowing up against the fence, the quality of the grass, dried bleached out gold light with the air and light of the tablelands in it, the quality of the air and wind blowing the dried grass against the fence, gathering the grass and then making it into a bed to sleep on, sleeping on the quality of air and light of that place. The air and light is what makes the tablelands. And the air and light is stitched into the words and the very simple story. I write the body/place story, the story of lemons, and it is only then that I can know, through the lemons. It is a practice of everyday life derived from thinking through Country, a methodology of lemons.

"Passing on of Knowledge" (Representation)

> If you can look at this painting in your mind's eye and strip away everything but the dots you are actually looking at hundreds of thousands of hectares of land. What is important here is that this is the way we passed on knowledge and whether the pictorial reflection was a sand drawing, cave painting, tree carving, message stick or the narrative of a ceremony dance, song, or music, this was the Aboriginal way of preserving knowledge and passing it on. We didn't have canvases, the variety of colours, or indeed paintbrushes as they are now, so we used what was here—wood, ochres, dye, dye from grass and plants, rocks, both for colour and for painting onto, the sand, fire, our own bodies and our voices to pass knowledge on. (Immiboagurramilbun)

For Immiboagurramilbun, the images held in her paintings constitute a symbolic language of the knowledge of Country. Knowledge of Country is not about a generalized entity such as "environment" or land, nor is it so human-focused as "place." It derives from a specific material landscape that has its own life force, energies, and connections, and embodies all that exists within it. It includes herself as a distinctive life entity, and the other beings who have shaped her multiple lives. The paintings are intended to communicate knowledge:

> from the Old People who walked this land, the first people
> from the spiritual lives of our own and other cultures
> from the spirit of nature
> from the deep knowledge of healthy
>   processes embedded in our bodies
> from a contemporary rhythm for personal,
>   social, and ecological transformation

In order to learn to think through Country I look at both the actual paintings and their digital images. I listen to the words that Immiboagurramilbun speaks to tell me about the paintings as I look at the images. I consider each of these separately, and then together, and learn quite different things from each aspect of this process. I bring to this analytical consideration my past history, my initial experiences of the country of the Narran Lake and of living in the desert, and my experience of other places. I write my response to Immiboagurramilbun, and to Country.

When I return to the DVD and listen to the precise words over and over as I look into the images, it is as if I have entered a portal, a threshold between two worlds, and I am back again in the desert where I lived at that remarkable time of the beginning of western desert art. For us this was an ordinary time in an ordinary life. My husband was a teacher, I was a mother with two, then three, children. The old men used to come to our house with crude artifacts or boards painted with the early symbols of western desert art to sell for a few dollars. Or they would turn up with their families when the rains came to camp on our lounge room floor and bring some painted boards with them. In hindsight, what was so significant about this time was the remarkable translation of Country into contemporary Western forms of representation through visual art.

It is in the space of this translation that I dwell when I look into the dotted landscape of the painting that Immiboagurramilbun calls passing on knowledge. The dotted patches of country remind me of moving through the desert landscape with its dotted foliage of different colors and shapes. She says that "each area of the painting" represented by different colored dots is "talking of a different knowledge" that would take longer than a thesis text to explain. A Gumbayngirr Elder from the east coast told me that in his country each dot represents a different creation story of a living being in the landscape and that there are creation stories for every living thing. Either way it is an extraordinary leap from the traditional ways of passing on knowledge of Country on bodies and ground designs in ceremony to painting on board and canvases. It is not only the process that marks an extraordinary leap, but the body knowing held in those mental images that translates deep knowledge of "hundreds of thousands of hectares of country" to a 3 foot by 4 foot board animated with color.

I think of Immiboagurramilbun's paintings now as ground designs of Country and self, the space of feet and dancing. They are like the designs painted on my white skin in red, yellow, and white ochre that told the story of Country in the desert.

> Body design. Touch. Earth on body. What is this art but earth on body? Where country touches me literally and stays between me and my clothes. A new skin.

As Grosz says of western desert artist Kathleen Petyarre's mountain devil paintings,

> each is becoming devil of paint itself, the coming alive of the patterns and corrugations of its skin, of its tracks, of the arcs of its movements, as well as the projection of skin onto the terrain, the belonging together of both the skin, the movement of the mountain devil over its terrain… and the earth and its secret locations, which sustains them all through its own excesses and their ingenuity. (Grosz, 2008, p. 94)

> As more profound than vision or hearing, rhythm (which we must understand, along with vibration, as another name for difference) is what runs from objects to organs, from organs to the objects that captivate them, and from their relations to the art objects that carry sensations. It is rhythm that is transmitted directly from universe to artwork to body and back. (Grosz, 2008, p. 83)

There is a patch of remnant rainforest near where I live now that represents a place of passing on knowledge of Country. It is a place of layered meanings that I have written about often. I have taken students there to learn body/place writing. It is located in a small mountain range that separates Latrobe Valley from the coast. A place of rainforest, creeks and valleys, high ridges and tall forest trees, it is a designated National Park. This means that this patch of country offers a place where everyone is free to go and learn about their part in the larger territory of the universe, of the more-than-human world. Being able to go there at any time of the day or night shapes identity in

Country for me in the small town where I live, nestled into the curved arm of this low mountain range.

Ten minutes away, I walk there for much needed escape from the grid of bitumen roads and suburban houses. At first, not knowing this country, I follow the map and signs in the interpretative pamphlet to guide my walk and tell me its stories. I learn its beginning story of Mrs. Ellen Lindon for whom it was also a meaningful place. She knew where the endangered ground orchids grow in that place and had it designated a National Park. "Lindon's Grove" is a marked stopping place with a picnic table in a cleared circular glade above a tiny creek that gurgles between rocks and tree ferns after heavy rains. The picnic spot is guarded by two tall mountain ash, and a dark brown wallaby grazes there.

I walk in this place often so I know it well. Every time it is the same and every time it is different. I breathe the deep green air of trees that make this place, the very air shaped by the tall mountain ash, so tall I can barely see their tops. Sometimes great branches crash to the forest floor and lie there creating worlds within worlds. Fallen red cedar remnants of the days of forest logging lie green mossed and ancient on the forest floor. Always sound all round of wind rustling leaves, bark-fall in long strips, bird song, and lyrebirds mimicking response. Deep throated territorial call of koalas rings out across the valley; crunch, crunch of gravel path underfoot, and in long hot summers, the crackle of leaf dryness in this land of fires. Trees that survived the last great fire bear its charred and blackened marks. I walk inside the scar of one old survivor, a black curtained cave, deep into the inner wound-world of tree. After rain damp air smells of eucalyptus and tiny ground orchids spring up bright pink amongst the green.

One Sunday morning in Spring I walk there at first light. A rock wallaby stands upright and still on the track in front of me. Body balanced on long tail and strong hind legs, paws poised in front of chest. I sense the texture of warm dark fur, changing shades of brown, gray, cream over back and underbelly. Ripple of light in fur with slightest muscle movement. Delicate nose, ears, and mouth twitching slightly; each of us responding to the other. He hops a little way and stops again to munch on leaf tips as I pass by. Up the hill a lyrebird sings, chirruping and trilling, mimicking all the other sounds, but with its song louder, more insistent, so I know it is a lyrebird. As I stand still to listen I come face to face with him only a few feet away. In that moment of recognition he begins to dance. He turns his back, dancing feathers facing me, and slowly raises the lyre-shaped tail. Fully open, he holds the lacy curtain of feathers aloft and quivers their pearly luminescence in the green shady light. A slow Sunday of little miracles.

Then one night of the moon in high summer, the forest is brooding with a kind of electrified intensity. It is late and the full moon is about to rise. Walking up the track all is waiting, watching. Up on the ridge in the direction of moonrise a lyrebird walks along thin branches high on a tall mountain ash. Usually on the ground, a dancer not a flyer, he cruises from branch to branch, tree to tree, walking and gliding, lyre tail silhouetted dark against fading light of sky. He tries one branch and then another as if profoundly unsettled, moving higher and higher on thinner and thinner branches, then a long slow glide to yet another tree. Koalas' deep throated calls echo back and forth across the valley sounding the air all round and nearby, tracking the sound to a single tree, a little koala climbs way up high and out onto the thinnest branch. We are all of us waiting for the moon. Out of the trees the full moon rises gold over cleared fields in concert with the minute by minute fading blue-green light of sky. Grass field now silvered I lie looking at the moon through dark patterns of leaves. I am summer grass bathed in silver light. I am tree glittered silver, leaf, trunk, and branches. I am white petal skin in moonlight. It is moon time in high summer.

In writing from these images held in the body I return to the foot, apple-belly, plum-baby, and forest-moon-walk to explore a methodology of thinking through Country. I write them in response to Immiboagurramilbun's being, knowing, and acting in the Country she belongs to, the country of the Narran Lake. I write them as a white immigrant settler woman with no place that I can call my Country. They are stories of the in-between where I can pause and find a resting place. However brief, however transient this pause in the place of writing is, this temporary home place, it is also forever, for all time.

Like the apple story, finding a place for that one new life, that one big round pregnant belly to split into two, a place that was safe, the one. This is finding a place for that new story, a new story of Country to come into being. Like Immiboagurramilbun's Narran Lake, water places are defined as places of creation, and simultaneously sites of representation, through which knowledge of Country is mapped and learned. They are also the site of this w/riting as creation and as a practice of Country from the space between self and other, self and country, self and the world.

Map 4: A Walking Water Story

4

A LITERATURE REVIEW OF WATER[1]

A Re-View of Country

The road between Cobar and Bourke, hundreds of kilometers south of the Narran Lake, stretches out endlessly, vast blue sky in front and behind. On each side of the bitumen intense red earth where the ground has been disturbed by graders. Against the red, yellow flowering bushes, shoulder-high, move in a light breeze. Closer to Mount Gundabooka, deep red earth more intense, color pressing into body. Gravel track off the main road leads into "the teaching place."

The track begins in shiny grasses waving silky feathers in the breeze. Walking between mulgas, casuarinas, and big round rocks, neat little metal signs with a curved rainbow serpent mark the way. It winds through stones and bushes, with distant blue hills between the trees, until we reach a creek gully. No water but piles on piles of massive red-brown rocks tumbling down the creek bed. Climb up the steep bank, weaving in and out of huge boulders, finally arrive at a long low rock shelter hidden among the boulders. Blocked. The whole rock overhang is bounded by a timber viewing platform and enclosed in a steel grid cage. Confronted by another enclosure. Work hard to overcome a sense of repulsion, knowing the fragility of ancient rock art and the need to protect it.

I am soon drawn into a world of dancing figures painted in ochre on rock. Curtains of fluted and ruffled rock surfaces lead in toward a deep internal space. Outside this inner core, layers and layers of rock surfaces face in all directions. On every layer there are groups of human and animal figures, all dancing. The figures are painted in white ochre that shines from the darkness. Only one is in deep red ochre, a Clever Man with a boomerang in one hand; his other arm, very long and extended, ends in an emu foot. The feet on the white emu figures are all pointing down, which is the pose of the father emu sitting on the nest. On another surface, in a row of dancing male figures and an emu, a single female figure gives birth. Further in, the pattern of the fish traps with a white ochre cod swimming toward them. As eyes get used to the dim light, deep inside a lower surface, a group of figures shine white on a background of red ochre near the white shape of the Narran Lake. These are differently shaped dancers, the white more intense in the darkness.

All the special water places are mapped here on these rock surfaces. Lorina Barker[2] says the cave at Mount Gundabooka is a teaching place where her Grandmother and Great Aunts told her the creation stories linked to the Narran Lake. Her Grandmother lived on the Barwon River near the Brewarrina fish traps, so her stories began at the fish traps that she called "Baiame's stepping stones into the heavens":

> Baiame created the fish trap and that story relates to a lot of the communities, a lot of the different groups of people because the fish traps—[the Creator] not only created the fish traps in Brewarrina, he also created Mount Gundabooka and he created a waterhole in Byrock [in] which he did his carvings and stuff. Then he moved, so he moved around the area and then he went to Brewarrina and created the fish traps and the fish traps are like his stepping stones back into the heavens.

The pattern of rocks at the fish traps are read as part of a storyline of special water places. While the rocks were placed by Ngemba people in this pattern and in a particular relationship to the flows of the river for the purpose of catching fish, they are also seen as the creator's net, flung across the river at the time of its creation. Similarly, the indentations in the rock at the edge of the river near the fish traps are the creator's giant footprint. It is another visible sign of the creator's presence and of the significance of this place in the creation storyline, "a sentence in the Aboriginal story." The creator made the drawings of the Brewarrina fish traps on the rock surfaces at Mount Gundabooka to teach the stories of the special water-story places hundreds of kilometers apart:

> [At Mount Gundabooka] there's pictures of the fish trap so there's a round sort of like stone pebbles drawing and a fish swimming into it and there's men with spears, there's a woman giving birth and there's animals and hand prints, yeah, and when I realised, then that's where you can see the connections. I mean over the years I think that's how I realised the connections between places, yeah, seein' that little fish trap painting on Mount Gundabooka was amazing.

Even as a contemporary young woman, Lorina was told by her Grandmother about Mount Gundabooka as a birthing place, the place of the last traditional birth. She told her about the special waterholes associated with birthing and the passing on of female knowledge. Although no longer used for birthing, they are where Lorina learnt the significance of personal and collective embodied connections to these important (water) places. Narran Lake, Brewarrina, Mount Gundabooka, and Byrock are all special water-story places that tell about significant events in the movements of the great ancestral beings across the landscape. Knowledge of Country and of water is passed on in stories told in oral traditions by older family members, in the signs and symbols of creation stories read in the landscape, and from the landforms of country itself. Together these constitute the body of literature that is read as the knowledge of water in this country. A literature review of water, in this sense, is a (re)view of Country. How, then, does this kind of knowing intersect with knowledge passed on through the written word?

Reading and Writing Global Water

When I move into the universalizing discourses of a conventional written literature review I lose my footing, I'm no longer grounded in any Country. In Australian Aboriginal understandings, Country is always specific; there is no generalized Country. When I write with Aboriginal collaborators, I am always in a specific place, multiple specific local places, moving through the landscape, walking, learning place. But I need to bridge the gap between the world of knowing through these places, rock paintings and oral stories, and knowing through reading and writing. Otherwise this knowledge remains in Country and cannot be learned more widely, cannot influence the canon of Western knowledge. What is the relationship between the act of reading and writing a "literature review" of water, and the flows of cultural knowledge of water in an oral, place-based culture?

Oral stories, like performance, ground, and body designs, are ephemeral, they blow away with wind and the passage of time. The symbols on the rock surfaces of the cave are more like ancient written texts. They are singular, more like art forms in their singularity. They are imbued with sacred power, made by the Creator to tell the story of water. Their meanings are only transparent to those with inside cultural knowledge. In other ancient cultures the symbols formed by the hands of their scribes were similarly powerful. They held the sacred laws governing the regulation of social and ethical behavior. Writing fixes things in ways that oral language does not. In a postindustrial culture of writing, knowledge is transmitted in mass produced print, and digital words proliferate endlessly in cyberspace. I wonder about the relationship between the black marks on a white page that fix meanings and the endless flux of knowledge in an oral story. I want to explore the different relationships to water embodied in different knowledge systems based in orality and literacy.

I have spent much of my academic career questioning the relationship between knowing through body/place connection and academic knowledge. The scene of this interrogation has always been writing. I do this through a practice of body/place writing to represent the translation of my own bodily experience into written text. I trace the movement from recorded oral stories to the written word. I teach my students to move between words, worlds, and knowledges through their experimental writing. Reading of academic texts has not been central to this long interrogation; it is almost as if it has been incidental to this work. I recognize this only now when trying to find a way to connect with the ideas generated through reading about water and struggling with claims about universal meanings. When I read, for example, that indigenous cultures all over the world have managed water in sustainable ways (Shiva, 2002), I understand this claim as a universalizing construct of Western knowledge. How can I trust generalized knowledge claims about indigenous cultures all over the world? Has Vandana Shiva visited all of the indigenous cultures of the world, dwelt in all of their places, walked in their countries, listened to their stories?

The universalizing power of scientific objectivity has a long history of critique by feminist theorists, notably Sandra Harding and Donna Haraway. In *The Science Question in Feminism*, Harding (1986) proposed a postmodern insistence on irreducible difference and affirmed the radical multiplicity of local knowledges. In response, Haraway agreed and further argued "for situated and embodied knowledges and ... against various forms of unlocatable, and so irresponsible, knowledge claims" (Haraway, 1988, p. 583). Despite decades of critique and the development of alternative methodologies, Western knowledge systems continue to value objective, abstract generalizations as the dominant form of legitimate knowledge. This has been further intensified under contemporary neoliberalism as globalization studies proclaim the end of the local in the age of the global (Appadurai, 1996).

In continuing the trajectory of this early feminist work, my interest is in understanding the nature of knowledge systems in which local, embodied knowledge is privileged and valued. How do these knowledge systems move to more general understandings without losing their necessary relationship to the local? I have explored the nature of local place-based knowledge in a series of projects in collaboration with Australian Aboriginal cultural knowledge holders and communities. I have asked a series of questions about the move from local to regional to global knowledges:

What is the nature of local place knowledge?
How do indigenous knowledge systems move from local to regional knowledges?

How do indigenous knowledge systems move from local/regional
to global knowledges without losing the material specificity of
the local?

In the first of these ethnographic projects with Gumbaynggirr people on the midnorth coast of New South Wales, we identified local
place knowledge through stories and practices of eating food, building shelters, and knowing spirit presences in local places (Somerville
& Perkins, 2010a). These stories and place practices have evolved in
cultural contexts in settled Australia, including their translations
into the English language. They are contemporary, dynamic relationships through which local places are named, inhabited, and loved. It
became clear in analyzing this local place knowledge that there were
also processes by which this place knowledge moves beyond the local.

In the second project, "Connecting the Dots" (Somerville & Perkins, 2010b) we traced, through detailed ethnographic research, how
this movement is structured. Using a method we named "deep mapping," we mapped the walking trails that are the basis of the lines of
story that travel across Gumbaynggirr country. These walking trails
link special story places where events in the epic journeys of the creation ancestors occurred. Together these stories and walking bodies
make connections across Country. Knowledge of linking trails is as
significant as knowing the special places and their stories. Together
they form a storyline or songline. This knowledge was ritualized in
initiation and increase ceremonies but even without the ceremonies
the knowledge continues to be passed on orally. The knowledge structures remain, albeit translated into contemporary forms through the
continuing work of language and cultural practice.

The third project, *Bubbles on the Surface* (Somerville, 2008b), was
designed to address the question of how indigenous knowledge
frameworks move from regional to more-than-regional (global) place
knowledge. It began with the specific local place of the Narran Lake
but was always underpinned by the idea that the Narran Lake is located
in the middle of a system of interconnected waterways. I had understood this through Chrissiejoy's concerns about the impact on the
Narran Lake of the damming of water for cotton irrigation at Cubbie
Station thousands of kilometers upstream. It is common knowledge

throughout the Murray-Darling Basin that the massive extraction of water in many sites along the waterways necessarily impacts on all of the waterways and country downstream. The means through which such understandings can be incorporated into knowledge systems grounded in Country is the question this work addresses.

Bubbles on the Surface was designed to understand what a study of the Narran Lake can teach us about water, and how we can incorporate its pedagogical possibilities into educational processes to ensure the protection of people and ecosystems. Reviewing the literature of previous research about water raises many questions in relation to these objectives. How can we know water? Is it possible to understand water as a global entity, separated from its spatial, temporal, and cultural contexts? What is this act of reading/writing water and how can it be contained without losing the flux and flow that water offers? How can we move between knowledge of water through reading and the flux and flow that characterizes oral place-based cultures?

I ponder this question in relation to leading global ethnographer of water Veronica Strang. In many works Strang (2004a, 2006a,b) has researched how people relate to water in different countries and contexts. She describes her approach as "material cultural analysis." Water, she writes, is "the most elusive and changeable of objects" which she seeks to understand as a phenomenological entity (Strang, 2006a,b, p. 70).

> Water is characterised, above all, by its fluidity, transmutability, and omnipresence. It is always on the move, flowing, conforming to the shape of its environment, evaporating and precipitating. Its form is equally inconstant; … It can be entirely invisible and transparent, or impenetrable and reflective. It shimmers with light and movement. (Strang, 2006a, p. 70)

In writing the story of water in a dry land I am interested in the possibilities of reading and writing an ethnography of water. What might a "thick description" of water entail? In order to write a literature review of water at all I have to make a shape, a container to hold the ideas of water. As Virgina Woolf noted of her efforts to capture the everyday flow of her relationship to her mother as part of everyday life, "I see myself as a fish in a stream; deflected; held in place; but cannot describe the stream" (Woolf, 1989, p. 90). In this review I am seeking a way to describe "the stream" through a series of temporary stopping places. I take up the three universal characteristics of water proposed by Veronica Strang: water as fluidity, water as omnipresence, and water as transmutable—to consider reading and writing an ethnography of water. I structure the following writing around these propositions as a series of (water)marks like the lines on the black rocks that mark the different levels of water in the Booralong Creek, or the lines on the sand made by the water's constant moving passage. Each water mark is a temporary stopping point in the flow of knowledge, momentarily separated out from the flow of the "unremarkable fabric of everyday life."

Watermarks: Thinking Through Water

Watermark 1: Water as Flow

> [Water] is always on the move, flowing, conforming to the shape of its environment. (Stranga, 2006, p. 70)

The question here is related to the 40 patches of different colored language territories that constitute the Riverine Language Group of the Murray-Darling Basin. How are the boundaries of these language territories made, and how does cultural knowledge move across these boundaries of country?

In coastal Gumbaynggirr country local place knowledge inheres in the most immediate local clan area. The language group territory as a whole is divided into five clan areas and each is the country that cultural knowledge holders have authority to speak about. It is where extended family groups walked and camped, gathered food and built shelters in their daily lives. They knew this country intimately from within their everyday experience and from stories passed on by their elders. In this way of knowing, a sense of identity, belonging and attachment to Country is constructed from within one's embodied connection and intimate daily knowledge of local places. Tony

Perkins· research collaborator and Gumbaynggirr coauthor (Somerville & Perkins, 2010) said:

We can put lots of dots on a piece of paper within a certain area, but outside that area you might find only a coupla dots, but they're more ceremonial type camping areas when you're travelling from one area to another.

Lines on a map, he said, "hem people in" because they are contrary to a sense of local country defined from within experiential and relational knowing. These lines do not conform to Country as it is understood through the delicate negotiations with others involved in boundary work.

Gumbaynggirr people moved through their country and across clan boundaries on walking trails. Knowledge of these linking trails was as significant as the knowledge of particular local places. The most extensive walking trails represent the highest form of cultural knowledge, crossing large tracts of country for travel to ceremonies on the edges of language group territory. These linking trails were hundreds of kilometers long and in Gumbaynggirr country travelers found their way through rugged gorges by directional stone arrangements placed on the highest mountain peaks and aligned with the stars of the Southern Cross. The linking trails were also the lines of story that followed the tracks of the creation ancestors connecting the story places. Like beads on a string each of these special places is linked to the other special places in the storyline.

In dry country, walking trails followed the lines of water sources, knowledge of which was essential for survival. In the drylands of the Murray-Darling Basin, for example, water and water pathways are "central to the way Aboriginal people speak about their land, and the many traditional stories about land are about networks of watering places" (Goodall, 2002, p. 39). The mound springs of the Artesian Basin provide a richly layered cultural route that "highlights the importance of water in determining lines of travel across the world's most arid continent" (Blair, 2001, p. 44). How the qualities of water as an element work in this cosmology was not open to me until considering this literature review of water, moving between Western and indigenous knowledge systems.

In what is described as "the new mobilities paradigm" (Sheller & Urry, 2006), it has become fashionable to think only in terms of mobility, and to lament the fate of the local in the age of the global (Appadurai, 1996). Other scholars, in defense of local place, have identified this trend to consign "place" to "the realm of the particular, the limited, the local and the bounded" (Escobar, 2001, p. 143) as a characteristic of Western philosophy. Lisa Malkki describes this way of thinking as "a sedentary metaphysics," related to the tendency of the modern Western world to locate people in particular spaces and within particular boundaries as the source of authentic identity. On the other hand, a "nomadic metaphysics" emphasizes only mobility, the transnational flow of people and commodities with fundamentally deterritorialized identities (Malkki, 1992).

It is water, however, in its quality as flow that can add significantly to understanding the relationship of the local and global in knowledge frameworks. Water constantly moves, shaping the contours of the land and the nature of knowledge. Water flows, that is its phenomenological nature: "So the use of water has escaped the legal and political boundaries established over either fresh river water or salt sea water, detaching it from political borders and giving a sense of it being once again 'a commons'" (Goodall, 2006, p. viii). Water as both a literal entity and a metaphysical phenomenon flows across countries, cultures, boundaries, binaries, disciplines, and genres, enabling the possibility of literal and metaphysical connections between them.

In thinking through Country and thinking through water, I ask, how are Country and water the same and how are they different? In asking this question and considering water as flow, I propose that it is water that is the mechanism whereby knowledge moves from local to regional to global in place-based knowledge systems.

Watermark II: Water as Omnipresence

As the substance that is literally essential to all living organisms, water is experienced and embodied both physically and culturally. The meanings encoded in it are not imposed from a distance, but emerge from an intimate interaction involving ingestion and expulsion, contact and immersion. Engagement with water is the perfect example of a recursive relationship in which nature and culture literally flow into each other. (Strang, 2004b, pp. 4–5)

Originally grounded in feminist poststructural thinking, my own research has long followed a trajectory of working between the binaries of nature and culture. Feminist poststructural thinking emphasizes the central role of language in the constitution of the human subject. In the burgeoning of feminist scholarship in second wave feminism a focus on the body was controversial because of the problem for feminism of the essentializing of women's bodies. A number of key feminist theorists, however, including Jane Gallop, Vicki Kirby, and Elizabeth Grosz argued against focusing solely on language and followed a path of the body as an important trajectory of research and thought. Liz Grosz's strategy to interrogate philosophy from the point of view of the body to destabilize the mind/body binary was central to this scholarship (see Grosz, 1994). My project has been to reinstate body/place connections in feminist poststructural thought.

A key site for Grosz's early theorizing was the insertion of the body into language. Lacan proposed that during the "mirror stage" the infant, previously connected to the mother and the body of the world as a total sensory being without language, was inserted into the symbolic order of language and representation. Parallel to her early work on Lacanian psychoanalysis, Grosz explored the writings of the French feminist philosophers Irigaray, Kristeva, and Cixous who variously theorized the site of the body's relationship to language, to patriarchal knowledge, and to the space of the mother.

I have taken up this theoretical space to explore body/place connections, giving primacy to materiality in analysis and to body/place writing. I have argued that to learn place through the sensing body is to learn about place differently (Somerville, 2010). The materiality of body/place connects the human body to the more than human world, including the corporeality of animals and plants as other living beings, and the "flesh of the world" (Merleau-Ponty, 1962). In this thinking I have proposed an alternative ontology based on "a reciprocal relationship with objects and landscapes, weather, rocks and trees, sand, mud and water, animals and plants, an ontology founded in the bodies of things" (Somerville, 2007, p. 234). The inclusion of the materiality of water adds a significant dimension to this thinking.

The human body is the first and most immediate cultural location of water. According to Western scientific knowledge, water comprises about three-quarters of the human body and is a major component of every cell (about 70%). Water is the essential basis of the human body's water-based systems. The circulatory, lymphatic, and excretory systems are dynamic fluid systems that circulate through the body and are essential for the maintenance of life. The amniotic fluid is the first environment for a human embryo, with all humans sharing the experience of their formation in its watery element. In the process of formation, the human embryo grows gills, a vestigial structure from the evolution of the human species from water dwelling creatures. While human bodies can survive for weeks without food, they can only live for a couple of days without water. Water is "the only material aspect of the environment that everyone, without exception, has to ingest and incorporate" (Strang, 2004b, p. 10).

How we understand bodies is culturally determined. For the Ninggirum people of Papua New Guinea the Ok Tedi River is the continuity of the water-body of the world that flows in and through human bodies (Oates, 2011). Ninggirum people's central creation myth tells how in the beginning there was only a rock and the creator urinated and defecated on that rock, thereby creating the substance of the earth and all of its waters. In their nonbinary system, urine as fluid is not abjected as in Western ontologies, but is the watery element that links human subjects into a collectivity, a body corpus. In Ninggirum culture urine is powerful and sacred as both inside and outside of the body. It is the means by which human bodies flow into and through other bodies of the world, linked to each other in a common corpus.

For Aboriginal peoples in Australia, Country is an overarching concept that includes water: "Country is multi-dimensional—it consists of people, animals, plants, Dreamings; underground, earth, soils, minerals and waters, surface water, and air" (Rose, 1996, p. 8). It is in focusing on the specific elemental quality of water as omnipresence, however, that we can extend our understanding of the intertwining of nature and culture through the body. Water moves in and through

Country and the bodies of all the living creatures that make up Country. In this, water is different from the other material qualities of the fabric of the world; not only is it part of all living bodies, but it moves in and through them in a constant cycle. Water, in this quality of omnipresence, can transform our understanding of how place-based knowledge systems can contribute to a different intellectual tradition.

In thinking through water as an essential constituent of all human and other-than-human living bodies, water functions as a literal and metaphysical connector between nature and culture. The exchange of water between and through human and all other living bodies intensifies the meaning of water as omnipresence on the metaphysics of knowledge systems.

Watermark III: Water as Transmutable

> Water is characterised [by] evaporating and precipitating. Its form is equally inconstant; it can transform from ice to fluid, to steam and back again. It can be entirely invisible and transparent, or impenetrable and reflective. It shimmers with light and movement. (Strang, 2006a, p. 70)

In rationalist scientific understandings the transforming and transformative cycles of water are understood as "the hydrological cycle." David Brunkhorst argues that the actions and choices of local human communities interacting with the ecological systems of the local landscape at different scales affect a "place" and give rise to its social identity (Brunckhorst, 2000, p. 35). He draws on the hydrological cycle to illustrate "the connectivity of nature through multiple scales of space and time":

> A single raindrop hits the earth at the scale of millimetres. Some will be absorbed into the soil, but many more similar raindrops create a puddle that is a metre or two across. Rivulets gather (10s of metres) and flow into small streams (kilometres), which in turn feed larger and larger rivers (100s kilometres), eventually to feed oceans (1000s kilometres) and evaporate to travel the global atmosphere as water vapour. (Brunckhorst, 2000, p. 17)

This form of theorizing makes considerable advances in considering the relationship between humans and the environment but rationalist, scientific knowledge cannot account for the ineffable, the transforming and transformative power of water that constitutes the sacred. It is precisely the transmutability of water that links water literally and metaphysically to birth, to death, and to sexuality, as the great dramas of human existence and understanding. The "hydrological cycle" contributes to our understanding of how the shape-changing nature of water is understood in scientific terms, but the deepest cultural knowledge of water is contained in myths and ritual practice. The term *myth* in the English language has the twin meanings of "a widely held but false belief or idea" and "a traditional story" (*Oxford Dictionary*), which is equally regarded with scientific skepticism. If we begin with the fundamental assumption that the epic storylines of the creation ancestors constitute knowledge, we have a different starting point for understanding water and its power in transformation.

Mythical stories embody the representation of the deepest cultural truths about water in language. Water is understood as the link between life and death in Christianity, Hinduism, and Buddhism, enabling new life after death (Oestigaard, 2006, pp. xx, 105). The "great fluvial myths of the Nile" convey cultural meanings about the transformation of the Nile basin in the cyclical return of the waters: "in the late spring, hope, prosperity, and verdure returned to the basin of the Nile born of the embrace between the moist Osiris and the earthy Isis" (Schama, 1996, p. 257). In the drylands of Australia, the mythology of the Rainbow Serpent embodies the transformative power of water: "the Rainbow Serpent rises up out of the permanent waterholes and starts travelling across the sky with the clouds that contain and release water ... [that] replenishes springs, rivers and underground water, people say, generating life and growth" (Rose, 2004, p. 39). Each of these cultural stories contains long and complex song cycles of the great dramas of human life and death, deep and ongoing stories of the relationship between humans and water in their different geographical and cultural/material locations.

These stories and song cycles are both universal and place-specific. While indigenous knowledge structures embody understandings of water as flow, as omnipresent and as transmutable, they have specific place-based meanings. These meanings inhere in language and naming, in the structures of thought that connect words in sentences to shape stories that connect to geographical locations. Specific cultural knowledge contained in the mythology of the Nile flood basin is not transferrable to the drylands of Australia, but the elemental nature of water informs each of them. Deep language work is required to understand the levels of translation and connection, materiality and metaphysicality, in different levels of meaning because there is no direct translation of deep cultural knowledge. Language as story is the primary site of embodied and embedded cultural understandings of water.

Through ritual the transforming qualities of water are incorporated into practice. Rituals of life and death involving water, such as baptism, initiation, and the cleansing and preparation of the body in death, are about transformation from one state of being into another. The meanings in myth and ritual practice are brought into being through the literal use of water and its metaphysical meanings. In many cultures the work of water in life and death is women's work, linked to their role in bodies and the procreation and sustenance of everyday life. Water in ritual enacts embodied practice that makes possible a liminal space in which deeper meanings and processes of life beyond rationality, logic, and words are incorporated into daily life and structures of knowledge.

In thinking through water, it is in its capacity to change form that it engenders the sacred. Its link to birth and death arises from the form-changing meanings of water, represented in myths and enacted in rituals in all religions and cultures of the world.

Water as Mutual Entanglement

Was anything left behind in the Nile? Is *that* the problem? That *nothing* was indeed left behind? Is this why, with Isis and Osiris reunited on the scrubby, muddy little island of Agilkia, something is wrong with the Nile? Polluted, evaporated, exhausted, it is dying. And it is hard to have faith, this time, in the resurrection. (Schama, 1996, p. 382)

The meaning of water as sacred, enacted in cultural knowledge through myth and ritual, struggles in contact with the dominance of scientific knowledge and practice. The deeply ironic contradiction in this lament is that the Nile, and the knowledge contained in its myths and rituals, can only be resurrected by the literal and metaphysical power of water. Water is indispensable and irreplaceable in its place-based materiality and specificity. The question must be then, how is it possible to move beyond the dominance of science and the hierarchical binary of nonindigenous/indigenous knowledge, in our thinking and practices of water?

In the struggle for recognition of indigenous knowledges globally, there continues to be an important political emphasis on the incommensurable differences between Western and indigenous knowledge systems (Tuhiwai Smith, 1999). In the case of water, however, where these differences meet, clash, merge and conflict, the maintenance only of difference through a reductive nonindigenous/indigenous binary is no longer tenable. In her ethnographic study comparing the meaning of water for villagers in Dorset, England, and indigenous peoples in Australia, for example, Strang found significant similarities in the meanings of water for the two groups. Each of these peoples was attached to their local water places and each was opposed to the commodification of their water for consumption. The English villagers, with their ancestral connections to the River Stour, are recognized as indigenous to the Celtic landscapes of their homelands. It is their similar indigenous connection to water that unites the English villagers and Aboriginal Australians. Everyone potentially has an indigenous relationship to water.

In tracing her family's 160-year connection with the land, Merill Findlay (2007) has recognized that a lifetime of personal memories and stories inextricably bind her to the Lachlan River in southeastern Australia. This sense of connection to the river is integral to her "very being-in-the-worldness." The recognition, however, is intensely discomforting because "the victor's" position involves stories that "explicitly exclude, silence, or subordinate the human and non-human 'others' who have been part of my life and the lives of members of my extended family for many generations" (Findlay, 2007, p. 309). The concept of mutual entanglement, proposed in the context of gifting cultures in the South Pacific, theorizes the ways that different cultures desire to know "the other" and are mutually implicated through the process. Mutual entanglement recognizes that "the story I am part of is one thread of a global web of stories about displacement and resettlement, dispossession and environmental degradation" (Findlay, 2007, p. 311).

Water is the literal and metaphysical site of "mutual entanglement" because of its capacity to cross boundaries of difference and of economic, political, spiritual, and environment domains of practice and thought. Water necessitates a reconceptualization of the contact zone to encompass more nuanced and complex understandings of human relationships than those structured within simply binary categorizations of nature/culture; indigenous/nonindigenous; self/other, self/world. Mutual entanglement involves an appropriate recognition of difference commensurate with the significance of water in socioecological meanings.

Water potentially plays a crucial role in moving beyond hierarchical binaries of thought that separate nature and culture, indigenous and nonindigenous precisely because of the qualities of flow, omnipresence, and transmutability discussed above. Through water we are mutually implicated with other humans, with more-than-human others, and with the fabric of the world. Stopping the flow of water in the world has an equal and opposite effect, it blocks the flow of cultural knowledge both literally and metaphysically.

Locks and Flows

Water in Australia involves the mutual entanglement of settler and migrant Australians with the oldest continuing indigenous culture in the world in the most arid inhabited continent on the planet. The model of regulated rivers around the world was replicated in Australia when rivers were forced to converge toward a desirable global standard for irrigation as a tool of imperial expansion (Sinclair, 2001, p. 65). In 1915, under the terms of the River Murray Agreement, the state and federal governments agreed to construct two large dams on the Murray River and 26 locks and weirs between the Murray's mouth and midriver at Echuca. The work was delayed due to the First World War but by 1939 15 of the proposed 26 locks and weirs were built, resulting in the most regulated river in the world (Sinclair, 2001, p. 67).

> Weir and lock No. 1 Blanchetown
> Weir and lock No. 26 Torrumbarry
> Weir and lock No. 3 Near Overland Corner
> Weir and lock No. 9 Lake Victoria Entrance
> Weir and lock No. 2 Below Waikerie
> Weir and lock No. 5 Near Renmark
> Weir and lock No. 11 Mildura
> Weir and lock No. 10 Wentworth
> Weir and lock No. 6 At State Border
> Weir and lock No. 4 Loxton
> Lake Victoria
> Weir and lock No. South Lake Victoria
> Weir and lock No. 15 Euston/Robinvale
> Mundoo/Boundary Creek Barrages
> Goolwa barrage
>
> (SINCLAIR, 2001, P. 68)

In a pictorial image produced by the Murray River Commission in 1946, the river was portrayed as "a giant elongated stairway," the straight lines across its width representing the locks and weirs that regulated its flow (Sinclair, 2001, p. 82). The smooth space of the flowing river is transformed into a territorialized, striated space of regulation and control (Deleuze & Guattari, 1987). The Barmah forest, a sacred place for the Yorta Yorta people, was one of the first and most obvious casualties of regulation. Important breeding grounds for ibis, heron, swan, and duck were lost resulting in the ever increasing menace of grasshopper plagues and massive problems of salination for agricultural enterprises (Sinclair, 2001, p. 70).

The discourses of neoliberal globalization present a contemporary variation to the discourses of modernity of the regulated river. Increasing demands for water from both urban interests and broad acre irrigation compete with a recognition of the urgent need for "environmental flows" because of the dire state of "the environment." "Current management arrangements for water have greatly reduced environmental values in many rivers ... native fish number only about 10 per cent of their pre-European populations in the Murray-Darling basin (Ladson & Finlayson, 2004, p. 19). The most common way to calculate the amount of water that should be released as environmental flows is described by one scientist in *"What's "Left Over," The Historic Situation in Many of Victoria's Rivers:* If the volume of water available for consumptive use is completely specified, and it is less than the total volume available, then the remainder could be considered to be the environmental flow" (Ladson & Finlayson, 2004, p. 20).

The authors note that while the concept of environmental flow might work in a year when rain is plentiful, under the more usual conditions of low rainfall, negligible water is available to maintain the life of the rivers. The current economic-based solution is water trading where federal and state governments buy back water for "environmental flows" from farmers with irrigation licenses. A series of angry protests have resulted from these policies. Fierce and heated demonstrations were held in 2008 and again in 2011 in response to the federal government's water buy-back schemes. The latest plan for the Murray-Darling Basin has reduced by half the amount of water originally identified as necessary for environmental flow. White privilege is especially hard to challenge within a discourse that equates the needs of the river to other consumptive requirements in a cultural regime that reduces all value to money.

Even more problematic, "Indigenous interests, practices, and uses in, or associated with, different waters have not been acknowledged in the current water reform agenda" (Altman, 2004, p. 30). It is important to recognize that Indigenous water practices need "to be considered, understood, valued and integrated into any emerging water property rights framework" (Altman, 2004, p. 30), but it may be that the gulf between water as a commodity to be owned and traded and Indigenous knowledge systems make such recognition impossible. Land rights and native title legislation in Australia have made important inroads into understanding practices of land but water as a literal and metaphysical entity in Indigenous cultures operates quite differently. Water, in itself, is fundamental to Indigenous ontologies and epistemologies and the destruction of waterways and water sources is equivalent to cultural genocide.

A fundamental paradigm shift is required in order that we learn to think about water differently. The question to ask then, is how to embrace the nature of water as a site of mutual entanglement to enable us to move forward in the knowledge that: "Sacred waters carry us beyond the marketplace into a world charged with myths and stories, beliefs and devotion, culture and celebration…. Each of us has a role in shaping the creation story of the future" (Shiva, 2002, p. 139).

Water, Art, and Emergence

> Art is the opening up of the universe to becoming-other. (Grosz, 2008, p. 24)

> A wonderful example of western desert Aboriginal art is Tali-Tali Pompey's *Anumara Piti* (Caterpillar Dreaming) which transcends coloured marks on a flat surface to become a commentary on movement and time, the colours of sounds lending themselves to shapes, as in a haunting painting by Ginger Wilkilyiri, showing the sound of moonlight hitting the ground at night. (Gibbons, n.d.)

The global discourses about indigenous knowledge and practices of water are discourses of loss. They describe the loss as dams have displaced millions of indigenous people and simultaneously blocked the flows of cultural knowledge. They enumerate the loss of indigenous cultures and languages globally at an even faster rate than the loss of species. The idea of indigenous knowledges being "lost" has been a dominant discourse since they were "found" by the West. It has equally been a dominant storyline in Australian identity. There have certainly been massive losses, and yet, in my own work I have learned that the Aboriginal peoples that I work with are simultaneously immersed in loss and recovery, as I am. In the long, slow and sometimes painful process of piecing together the knowledge that remains, cultural knowledge and stories are being translated, transformed, and made anew. This is inevitably a process of mutual entanglement in which the forces of colonization are embraced in order to move forward.

In writing *Landscape and Memory* Simon Schama poses the question of loss in order to search for "a way of looking; of rediscovering what we already have, but which somehow eludes our recognition and our appreciation. Instead of being yet another explanation of what we have lost, it is an exploration of what we may yet find" (Schama, 1996, p. 14). Finding, however, is not an easy process. Kim Mahood (2008) asks this same question about loss in the confronting colonial context of the Australian inland, haunted by old Bessie's lament: "When I'm gone there'll be nobody left to talk to the lake in its own language":

> And so it must have happened by increments across the continent, that slow withdrawal of voices, the silence falling as the conversation between people and country lost the languages in which it could be spoken. Did the ancestors lie in the hills and watercourses, waiting to be called, wondering at the unfamiliar sounds that suggested something new and strange was taking place? Did they fade and disappear without the songs and ceremonies to invoke them, or are they waiting still? (Mahood, 2008, p. 169)

When something is lost, how can it be found again? Does it go underground like the Rainbow Serpent and come up again in a different place? How can we simultaneously acknowledge loss and presence? Mahood says: "There's a shiver of movement far out on the lake, a muscular convulsion that reaches the shore in a slow wave as the old snake turns in its muddy bed acknowledging Bessie's homage" (2008, p. 169). The libidinous surface of these words materializes the rhythms of country in the muscular convulsion of "the old snake." The Rainbow Serpent, like the invisible water of the drylands is omnipresent, inhabiting living and nonliving entities, the corporeality of the world. It is a story of the transmutability of water, its ability to change form and move across languages and cultures. The Rainbow Serpent appears as Mutagatta's bubbles on the surface of the deepest waterholes in Muruwari stories; as the pattern of desert sandhills made by the Ngatyi in Paakantji country; and as Kurreah whose thrashing made Terewah, the Narran Lake in Immiboagurramilbun's U'Alayi language creation story.

In *Chaos Territory Art* Elizabeth Grosz articulates a new theory of art. Following Darwin, Grosz argues that in sexual reproduction an excess is produced over and above the requirements of survival of the fittest. This excess is the origin of art. Living bodies draw from the chaos of the earth "to extract from it something not so much useful as intensifying, a performance, a refrain, an organization of color or movement that induces art" (Grosz, 2008, p. 3). This roots art in the "superfluousness of nature, in the capacity of the earth to render the sensory superabundant, ... The haunting beauty of birdsongs, the provocative performance of erotic display in primates, the attraction of insects to the perfume of plants, are all in excess of mere survival" (Grosz, 2008, p. 17).

Art draws from the erotic energy of the unformed chaos of the world by making a frame. In this act the body is joined to the chaos of the earth through the pause enabled by the frame. The libidinous energy of chaos also serves to disrupt the frame as art breaks through systems of enclosure to enable something of the chaotic outside to reassert and restore itself in and through the body: "painting aims to make every organ function as an eye, if it aims to make the very entrails see and look ... the body is, for a moment at least, directly touched by the forces of chaos from which it so carefully shields itself in habit, cliché and doxa (Grosz, 2008, p. 23). Through art we can temporarily stop the flow of water to articulate its meanings (in watermarks, in representations) in a way that continues to borrow from, and to enhance, the libidinous energy that inheres in water. It offers a means by which representations can work as flow, rather than stasis.

Here I return to the cave at Mount Gundabooka, to the question of what constitutes a literature review of water in a place-based oral culture, in order to bring these strands together. The cave is a teaching place of water; of fluidity, omnipresence, transmutability, and entanglement. Ceremonial places in this country are places of water, and ceremony is story, dance, ritual, and Country. The images on the surfaces of the cave map connections between water places hundreds of kilometers apart in different countries.

The cave is a place of mutual entanglement where outsiders can learn with a track, signs, map, and enclosure that signals its (post)colonial meanings. The cave is a place of excess, with its abundance of dancing figures shimmering in white ochre on its multicolored rock surfaces, "transforming the lived body into an unliveable power, an unleashed force that transforms the body along with the world" (Grosz, 2008, p. 24). It is a place of becoming-other through human transmutation of form, "the opening up of the universe to becoming-other."

Map 5: The Narran Lake

5

Intimate Intensity

Immiboagurramilbun (Chrissiejoy Marshall)[1]

I don't remember a time
without the Lake.
There were times
when it dried back
but they were quite rare
it was always full
and in season there'd be
thousands and thousands
of birds
you would wake up
in the morning
to birds getting a fright
taking off
and making a terrible clatter
then going to sleep
of a night time,
listening to all the birds
that lulled chatter
that you hear
of an evening.

Chrissiejoy Marshall

Chrissiejoy came to the University of New England in January 2000 to enroll in a PhD program. She supplied the usual documents, among them her birth certificate.

> Born: March 9, 1951
> Female A
> Mother: died March 9, 1951
> Father: Station Owner

I sensed in these few words of identity a big story that would gather me up in its momentum, but I had no idea of what would emerge. As a police officer and Aboriginal Advocate her time with me was punctuated by frequent and traumatic calls on her mobile: someone has been raped, someone else's children are being removed from their care. I wondered how she had the fortitude to take on all of this pain and suffering, but that was her other life. My work was to facilitate the bringing of her worlds into words through her doctoral research. She became a much loved part of a doctoral group that met once a year for an intensive week-long residential school. Her experience of previous university study had left her scarred in the struggle against the domination of Western knowledge frameworks. Her writing was moralistic and often angry, caught up in the savage binaries of Aboriginal identity politics. We tussled. She was a strong woman and I quickly grew to love her sharp tongued assertiveness and determination to have her say.

Everyone in the group was transfixed when Chrissiejoy did her performance at doctoral school. The first year she just listened, the second year she talked about way-finding, using the analogy of traveling home from the school the year before. She had taken the infamous Kempsey Road to travel from the top of the tablelands to the sea level plains below. Its gravel surface was slippery and the road winding and narrow, hugging the cliff face on one side and dropping hundreds of meters into the gorge on the other. The road was so narrow that if a car came in the other direction, there was nowhere to pass each other. Each car had to stop and work out how to reverse or inch forward to find a tiny curve that allowed the two to pass. Each hairpin bend was like driving over a precipice with no sense of what might be beyond it, or whether a car might appear in the other direction. Impatient drivers stick to your tail, brakes start to burn out from sitting on them to stop the momentum of the steep slope, and in these dry times the dusty road surface coats the windscreen making visibility difficult. This was the analogy Chrissiejoy chose to describe her experience of doctoral study.

The next year her performance was about something quite different. She began: "Margaret challenged and extended my intellectual boundaries, she saw the need for me to divert from conventional discourse and allowed me to develop my own form and content." I can recall the sense of power and command as she stood in front of all of us and proceeded to unfold the new "form and content" presented through a series of paintings and stories. Chrissiejoy performed her new methodology that we came to call "thinking through Country." Sometime in the process of being taken into the hearts of all the others in our doctoral group, and through beginning to trust that I was not about to reshape her with written words that erased all that she had experienced and believed in, she underwent a profound transformation in her relation to the academic world. This performance set our relationship in an entirely different direction. I visited the Narran Lake in all of its seasons, 500 kilometers due west of the office where we sat and talked, becoming intimately attached to the Lake through Chrissiejoy's memories.

Immiboagurramilbun grew up by the lake with her Noongahburrah Grandfather and Uncles and her Erinbinjori Grandmother. Her Grandmother had been taken captive as a young woman in her Erinbinjori country in the Gulf of Carpentaria on the far north coast of Australia. All of her people were massacred at the time, but she was young and beautiful. She was led the thousands of kilometers down through the channel country tied by a rope to white men on horses. They traveled like this until they reached Dirranbandi, near the country of the Narran Lake when the young woman fell ill with influenza. She was abandoned in the bush, left for dead. The Noongahburrah mob from the Narran Lake found the seriously ill young woman and one of the men, having just lost his wife, believed that this was a spirit woman sent to replace her. He nursed her back to health in their camp by the Narran Lake and it was there, by the lake, that Immiboagurramilbun's Mother, Karrawanna, her Grandmother's only child, was born.

Chrissiejoy says her Grandmother "would never talk, she never talked very much about the whole thing," but she saw the scars on her wrists from where the rope was tied. She said to me, "Can you imagine being dragged away having watched most of your people being slaughtered and probably believing that you're the only one left?" Chrissiejoy especially grieved for her Grandmother's loss of a community of language speakers, "Imagine that you're the only human being left, that you couldn't speak the language or know anybody, no one could speak, even the other Aboriginal people that she met on the way, no one could speak her language." Somehow her life went on, sustained by the lake.

They continued to live their daily lives there by the river and lake. The lake was now totally enclosed by white properties with fences marking their boundaries, cutting across the lake. The property where they lived was Boorooma, 124,000 acres, with the lake occupying anywhere between 5 and 15,000 acres of that property, depending on the season. When empty it grew abundant grasses and cattle were grazed there. The white property owner brought them supplies in an old Jeep once a month. The child who was born to the Erinbinjori Grandmother and the Noongahburrah Grandfather grew up and she became pregnant to the white property owner. Fearing that the baby would be taken away because of the color of its skin, the Grandmother made another long journey. She took her pregnant daughter and traveled 500 kilometers to Glen Innes on the New England Tablelands, just north of the University where we sat in my office exchanging stories.

Chrissiejoy rarely spoke her Mother's name. The story of her Mother was told in just a few words, "She died in two hours of me, she just bled to death." The new baby was born and through her Mother's last wish, her Westernized name was "Chrissiejoy," the joy of new beginnings. The grieving Grandmother brought the baby back to live in the camp by the Narran Lake. Chrissiejoy's white father registered the new baby, an unusual act for any child born outside the sanctity of Western marriage laws of the time, and when "half-caste" children were in danger of being taken by Welfare. Chrissiejoy points out that the birth certificate had an "A" beside the word "female" to mark her Aboriginal identity: "It was quite extraordinary actually, I'd walk down the street with my Dad and I'd be his daughter and that was it, his daughter full stop. And then I would walk down the street with Yoongalarlin[2] and I'd be, you know, a little black kid, yeah." Her Grandmother always carried the birth certificate with her. Chrissiejoy said she often thought about how her Grandmother would watch her ride off to school every day, and every time she went away the Grandmother could never be sure that her granddaughter would return.

Immiboagurramilbun's representation of her identity is the substantial achievement of a lifetime of identity work. The power of this story explains the deep significance of the painting *Me, Myself and I*, in its struggle to bring the strands of this story together. Dark red-brown painted masonite cut into multiple curves forms the ground for Immiboagurramilbun's telling of her selves. The color of desert earth, it is more like a patch of country than a painting as it lies on my lounge room floor. In the center of the patch of country there is a series of concentric circles with five differently patterned petals, or leaves, radiating outwards from the circles. I lay it on my lounge room floor to look more closely, a ground design of country and self, like the designs painted on my white skin in red, yellow, and white ochres that told the story of country in the desert. Around the edges each curve shelters an animal, a track, or a sign, all symbols through which Immiboagurramilbun understands the story of her identity.

The circle in the center is the same symbol that Immiboagurramilbun uses for the Narran Lake. In this painting the circle is also the symbol for her self. It is not blue, but equal thicknesses of dark and light concentric circles that form the shape of her selves. It is not clear when looking at these concentric circles whether the lighter ones are formed by the dark, or the darker ones are formed by the light. Each forms and shapes the other. She tells me that the five lighter circles show the five lives that she lives, they are "the Niddeerie [the ongoing creation story] of each one." These lives include *Yowee*, inner spirit;

Doowee, dream spirit; *Kungullun,* secret mind; *Mullowil* shadow spirit; and *Mullojel,* the connectiveness to ancestors and Mulgury. The darker circles are the Niddeerie of others connected to her so that "the whole of history is there."

Through the symbols sheltering in the curves around the edges of the painting Immiboagurramilbun recites the Niddeerie of the others who make up her identity. The first is the swans for her Mother and the Noongahburrah people of the Narran Lake. The second symbol is the Crocodile, from her Grandmother's country of the Erinbin-jori people of far North Queensland on the Gulf of Carpentaria. The Wardook/Bohrah (kangaroo) is for the men, and the Jindi/Dinawan is in the Belin (Rose, 2000) and Mulgury of the women. The Bandabee (kookaburra) symbolizes the Mulgury of her Grandmother, and the Albatross the Mulgury of her Son. Each of these symbols is linked by a trail of dots to show how they are connected to each other. The closeness of the dots indicates the intensity of their connections to Immiboagurramilbun's being, an ontological reality realized through the different countries, people, and life forms that make up those places.

In March 2005 after we received funding for our future work together about the Narran Lake, I sat with Chrissiejoy in her house in Granville in Sydney's western suburbs in a completely darkened room. As a result of the intense pain from her spinal injury Chrissiejoy had begun to have frequent severe migraine headaches, often requiring hospitalization and injections of pethidine. This left her shaken and overly sensitive to light and sound, gripping onto what little reality she knew before another migraine hit her. Despite her pain she was enthusiastic to go ahead with our project so I traveled to Sydney and visited her three times over a period of two weeks to record her stories.

There in that dark and airless room I sit with this woman whom I have so grown to love, and think about this story of unimaginable pain and suffering. There was the Grandmother who witnessed the killing of her people and experienced atrocities too terrible to speak of at the hands of the white men on horses. The Mother who fled to a place far distant from her home in case her baby was taken away. The daughter who has taken on so much trauma of others, who holds their pain in white crescent moon shaped scars in her brain. I have sobbed with Aboriginal women watching the film *Lousy Little Sixpence* when the mother runs after the train that carries her children away. I know the loss of children. I have listened in silent, breathless horror when Catch Ellis told of the shooting of women for performing ceremony as late as the 1960s (Ellis & Bochner, 2002). I have listened to my Gumbaynggirr collaborator talking with me about the Red Rock massacre story, again and again, slowly over years to try to understand. Never has it been so traumatic and so close to my heart as this.

> For if I am confounded by you, then you are already of me, and I am nowhere without you. I cannot muster the "we" except by finding the way in which I am tied to "you," by trying to translate but finding that my own language must break up and yield if I am to know you. You are what I gain through this disorientation and loss. This is how the human comes into being, again and again, as that which we have yet to know. (Butler, 2004, p. 49)

All I can do is to listen with "exquisite care and attention" as an act of love (Rose, 2000). To sit with this profoundly moving story and listen. And each time I ask for another story there is a long pause as Chrissiejoy travels back in time and place to the rhythm of their daily life by the lake. It is the lake, in all its rhythms and cycles, that has given her the strength to endure.

> The lake had to dry back
> we understood
> that it had to dry back
> to let the land breathe
> it was a seasonal thing
> the lake would come back
> when it was dry
> you did other things
> that was when
> the emus put their nests
> out on the lake bed
> before that you'd have to

go up into the ridges
but when it was dry
they were all out on the lake bed.

As a child I wished
the lake was back
like any kid
but you'd know that
the land had to have
time to breathe.

Terewah, Narran Lake

Millinbu was always the first
to come back.
Day to day frogs
they're called *yuwiya*
but when you talk about them
as our educator, teaching you
when the lake was coming back
they were called *millinbu*
Millinbu would come out
of their wet slime
smell the rain when it's coming
and they had to be up
and above the ground
before the water started.

The animals you'd hear them
coming back
the frogs would start to croak
of a night
and you'd hear them coming
days and days before the rain
you knew it was coming.
When the lake drove back
there'd be huge cracks
in the ground
and all those cracks
would all have to get filled
before you got a sheet of water
on top.

Sometimes it takes weeks for the rains to gather across the flood
plains and flow down the river, making its way across the dry cracked
ground. The lake has its cycles and seasons of wet and dry like many
inland waterways. They are what makes the lake so productive, such a
rich source of life, and food. In a normal cycle the lake would be full
of water for about 7 of 8 years, it would gradually dry back, shrinking
back from its plenteous watery edges until the whole expanse was dry
ground. When the ground was dry it was highly productive because
of the amount of decaying organic matter that had lived in the water.

Grasses would grow, rich and fertile, feeding the kangaroos, wallabies, emus, and all of the other creatures of the land that lived there. Then when the waters returned the grasses would die and then decompose, unable to survive under water. The decomposing organic matter made the watery environment a fertile place for the frogs and fishes, mussels and shellfish, and all the other watery creatures that were waiting to come to life. Migratory birds, also able to follow the return of the waters, would start flying in from other places to feed on the abundant life, to nest and produce eggs and young chicks in profusion.

We lived by the lake, as in we not only lived right there on the lake, but we lived by the seasons of the lake. How we ate, what we did, would continue throughout the seasons on the lake. It all depends on the lake and what was happening with it. You could smell the birds, and in different seasons it would have different smells. The smell of the birds and just the water in the wind give it that different smell. Yeah, you could smell the lignum.[4] Times when it was drying back we would be going to hunt for emus' nests out on the lake bed, in the lignum. Even in flood times, when we couldn't go to school 'cause you couldn't get across the vast swampland to get to the roadway, it was good fun. The lake dictated what happened in our lives.

The black swans were always there. Even before the lake, it was always Terewah home of the black swan. They were part of the lake and the lake was part of them. They owned the land, to us we belong to it, they have more right to it than we did because they were there first. They made their nests, raised their chicks in the lignum. The lignum needed the lake to survive but the lake needed the lignum too. The lignum sat above the water so a lot of the birds' nests'd be in the lignum. It was a huge part of the lake. Times when it was drying back we would hunt for emus' nests in the lignum out on the lake bed.

On the weekends we went musseling and we got more mussels than we could eat. We would put them in a hessian bag and put 'em back in the river, tied, and then pull them out later on and eat them, cook them on the fire, in the ashes, yeah, they just open up. I think Yoongarlin used to make a soupy stew stuff out of them too, but we used to just usually cook 'em up on the fire, you know, in their own juices. There was yabbies, lot of yabbies, fish, goanna, and snake and stuff like that there, especially if the men got one when they were out working, they'd bring one home. Emu eggs, used to eat a lot of emu eggs. Wild orange, quandong, wild lime, and little bush apples, yeah, in the seasons, wild oranges you could smell.

For Immiboagurramilbun's Grandmother who had traveled there from so far away in such traumatic circumstances, and for her Grandfather and Uncles who belonged in that country, it was the seasonal drying and return of the waters that sustained their life by the lake. It not only allowed them to survive, providing food, fresh water, and a place to make a camp by its shores, but it became a place to shape a new life and new cultural stories. Chrissiejoy's father made a decision not only to allow this small group of people to stay in their country, but he provided supplies once a month to their camp. As Chrissiejoy grew older her father taught her all of his Western knowledge about the cycles of the lake as she drove around the property with him. He especially taught her about the migratory birds, telling her where they came from, which birds nested where, their breeding and feeding habits. He was deeply attached to the lake and in her teenage years Chrissiejoy could remember him amassing evidence to have the area declared a Nature Reserve for its protection. One of the strongest early motivating forces for our work together was to retrieve this white acknowledgment of the significance of the lake.

Immiboagurramilbun's painting of the Narran Lake is different from all of her other paintings. She describes it as "finding and knowing place of self and others in Country." Unlike her more typical muted ochre colors, this one is gaudy pinks, greens, yellows, oranges, and blues, the brightest and most energetic of all the paintings. In the center, against a background of patches of country marked by different colored dots, a bright pink circle is outlined in blue dots with inner concentric circles of blue. The digital image of this painting, and this one alone, has an extraordinary quality. The dots which make up the shapes and form of the painting shimmer and move, as if animated by the energy of the lake's waters. I read these concentric circles in the painting's center as the intertwining of self and other, each shaping and forming the other through Niddeerie.

Outside the circles four pink snakelike shapes flow outward to the four corners; at the same time the eye is drawn toward the center. These wavy snake shapes are not quite connected to the center, except when the shimmer of blue dots that outlines their form merges with the blue dots around the center circle. The shimmer animates the connections of form and being to each other and to Country; bright green treelike forms also stretch out in all the directions of the painting. They are wavy childlike stems and leaves with small red and orange fruit along the stem. Around the treeleaf stems, fat shiny white bodies of witchetty grubs are scattered across this country, with the symbols of seated figures and their camps nearby.

In the epicenter of the painting, in the center of the circles, a pale pink eye shape with a blue-lined iris gazes out at me. Chrissiejoy's relentless gaze meets mine as I look into her painting. This eye/I center is also the blue of the Narran Lake, when the waters arrive and life returns.

The lake was always a place of story and representation. Chrissiejoy said: "It wasn't only a place to supply us with food, it was this bunker of knowledge that you had." They were told about the different parts of the lake and the events that had happened there during its creation. Some deep parts of the lake were taboo, they could never go there. The knowledge about the lake and these places of taboo were told in story. Chrissiejoy tells these oral stories and she also creates images through which to convey the ineffable meanings of the ancient stories of water. She talks about Kurreah, the giant lizard who created the Narran Lake, and draws on scientific knowledge as well as her Noongahburrah stories. She insists that Kurreah actually translates as "giant lizard." In the drawings done by the Old People in the ground, Kurreah is portrayed as a huge goanna with very sharp teeth and long claws. This creature, she tells me, is the same as the recently discovered fossilised skeleton of *Megalania Prisca*, an enormous, carnivorous, goannalike reptile, said to be about 8 to 10 meters long and weighing between 600 kilos and a ton, with razor sharp teeth and claws. This scientific knowledge provides proof for Chrissiejoy of the ancient and undeniable truth of the mythical story.

The first stories are almost beyond my memory. I grew up knowing the stories so I'm guessing that I was told as a very, very small child. When you first get told about the creation of the lake and Kurreah and how all that connects it's a very simplistic story, it was just simply that this huge animal was, you know, kept the kids away from the water holes because, "look out Kurreah'll get you." It was a story to keep you safe and then later on it gets deeper and deeper, so it's the same story but it just gets more detailed. As a tiny, tiny child you probably didn't even understand really that it was Kurreah that created the lake, it was more about he swallowed people and if you went too close to the water, the deep water, he might be still there, he might get you. Later on you get told about the creation story and then further on than that you get told about how they killed him and how he is now called upon as the spirit to make things grow. Yeah, it was probably one of the first stories I was told.

They talk about Baiame who is the Creator. He was here on earth and he had two wives, and he sent his wives to go and dig yams while he went to do something else, I think it was gather honey or something, and they were to meet at this waterhole. Anyway he got to this water- hole and the wives were missing, so he figured out what had happened to them and tracked them. He got around in front of it and it was Kur- reah, he had swallowed his two wives. So he waited in ambush and killed and slit open the belly and got his wives out. He put them on an ants' nest and brought them back to life and everyone lived happily ever after, but whilst he was killing the giant lizard, Kurreah swished his tail around and knocked the big hole in the ground and all the water he had swallowed flowed into that hollowed place that then became the lake. Baiame said, that in honour of Kurreah it would always refill with water and there would always be water and many birds and things there. So the birds were always there and as a resting place for them and as a place for them to come to breed, when they were going from one place to another, this was a really good place for them to stop over.

The lake was not only created by Kurreah, creation was formed at the lake. So, not for just Noongahburrah people or even so much just people speaking the language, it was also to other groups around there, a very important place and accepted as a place of creation. Narran Lake is the center of creation so for Noongahburrah people or for the people that spoke U'Alayi, they believed that Baiame, who is the Creator, started creation at Narran Lake, that area, that was the creation. Although Kurreah created Narran Lake itself, later the area that is now the lake was the area of creation, and so that's where he, the Creator, for want of a better word, came down to earth. So that was where Noongahburrah would invite other nations to come to do ceremony on the lakes.

The creation stories of the landscape and its waterways were collected by early settlers who had an interest in these stories of Country. Katie Langloh Parker, an early pioneering settler woman who lived on a large station in the Angledool area, collected and translated these mythical stories from the local Aboriginal people in the early days of white settlement. They are now published as "sacred texts" on the Internet. While the traces of white colonialism influence her translations, her early work in collecting and translating the creation story of the Narran Lake adds to its richness. In Langloh Parker's story "old Byamee," the Creator goes off to gather some honey and his two young wives go off in another direction to collect yams and frogs. They swim in the waters of a forbidden spring fed waterhole and they are swallowed by two "kurreahs"[5] who lived in the deep underground water.

> Having swallowed the girls, the kurreahs dived into an opening in the side of the spring, which was the entrance to an underground watercourse leading to the Narran River. Through this passage they went, taking all the water from the spring with them into the Narran, whose course they also dried as they went along.
>
> Meantime Byamee, unwitting [about] the fate of his wives, was honey hunting. He had followed the bee with the white feather on it for some distance; then the bee flew on to some budtha flowers, and would move no further. Byamee said, "Something has happened, or the bee would not stay here and refuse to be moved on towards its nest. I must go to Coorigel Spring and see if my wives are safe. Something terrible has surely happened." And Byamee turned in haste towards the spring. When he reached there he saw the bough shed his wives had made, he saw the yams they had dug from the ground, and he saw the frogs, but Birrahgnooloo and Cunnunbeillee he saw not. He called aloud for

them. But no answer. He went toward the spring; on the edge of it he saw the goomillahs of his wives. He looked into the spring and, seeing it dry, he said, "It is the work of the kurreahs; they have opened the underground passage and gone with my wives to the river, and opening the passage has dried the spring. Well do I know where the passage joins the Narran, and there will I swiftly go."... On swiftly sped Byamee, making short cuts from big hole to big hole, and his track is still marked by the morilla ridges that stretch down the Narran, pointing in towards the deep holes. Every hole as he came to it he found dry, until at last he reached the end of the Narran; the hole there was still quite wet and muddy, then he knew he was near his enemies, and soon he saw them. He managed to get, unseen, a little way ahead of the kurreahs. He hid himself behind a big dheal tree. As the kurreahs came near they separated, one turning to go in another direction. Quickly Byamee hurled one spear after another, wounding both kurreahs, who writhed with pain and lashed their tails furiously, making great hollows in the ground, which the water they had brought with them quickly filled. Thinking they might again escape him, Byamee drove them from the water with his spears, and then, at close quarters, he killed them with his woggarahs. And ever afterwards at flood time, the Narran flowed into this hollow which the kurreahs in their writhings had made. (Langloh Parker, 1897)

This creation story that Immiboagurramilbun grew up with, the earliest story of her memory, is the surface level of the knowledge of Country and water imparted through story. It is the level that would be told to children and the uninitiated and its most superficial meaning is a warning to protect the spring water that bubbles up from the deep underground waterways in the rock far below. In Muruwari language the "Rainbow Serpent" is called Muttagatta. The bubbles that appear on the surface of the deep waterholes signal the dangerous presence of the Muttagatta and render swimming in the waterhole taboo. The water that bubbles to the surface in springs, and the knowledge of the water through these stories, is crucial for survival in this hot dry country.

The flood plains of this country, where the waters flow down from the upper rivers in the Murray-Darling Basin, are rich gray soil, carrying the fertility of the flood plains. The dry "morilla" ridges of red earth are watered only by the springs that come from the artesian basin from water that seeps there over millions of years. The cycles of wet and dry are an essential part of the stories of this country, both for European farmers and Aboriginal people. In Western frameworks this is described as a cycle of "boom and bust" where fast money can be made from the riches of the flood plains when the waters arrive, and as they recede cattle are sold off and a "drought" mentality reigns. For the Noongahburrah people of the Narran Lake, the proper rhythmical cycles of the seasons of the lake and its life forms are essential to life itself. Their cultural stories depend on the cycles of wet and dry and the integrity of the underground waterways, so heavily mined for water in this dry land.

Dormant

I guess my memories of that,
to know where it's come from
to now
is the terrible part
because most of the lignum
has been ripped out,
it's almost like you can see
a vast nothing.
I've got a vision in my head
of how it was when I was a child,
and it's not that way anymore,
the water never gets there now.
Do I really want to go back there?

It's like when people are in grief
and you talk to them about
do they want to see the body
after someone has died
because it's completely different
especially after an autopsy
sometimes you think yeah
it would lay it to rest,
the concern that it is so different
now,
then at other times you think no
I just want to keep in my head
the way that it was.

In September 2006 some of the artists and myself traveled to Lightning Ridge to find the real Narran Lake. Chrissiejoy decided to join us there, determined despite the ever-increasing crescent moon shaped lesions, each representing another scar in her brain. She has been losing speech and mobility, walking with a stick, and speaking slowly and with difficulty. At night I dream that the moon shaped lesions are the crescent moon shining over the waters of the lake. Chrissie-joy meets us, as promised in her determined fashion, on the property "East Mullane" owned by the National Parks and Wildlife Service, the closest place to the Narran Lake.

It is a flickery, breezy sort of day with a hot dry wind. Eucalyptus leaves sparkle in the light. A flock of large black birds, ungainly like black cockatoos, fly from one small tree to another and chime in wind and flicker of light, up and down the scales, chiming through this thin light air. Butterflies flutter around sweet smelling white cedar in front of the old homestead. Immiboagurramilbun tells us this is a sign that we are welcome here. In late afternoon the shadows grow longer across bare pink dirt and in the early morning new tracks of birds and animals are printed in the red earth.

The house is a simple rectangular box built of fibro surrounded by wide verandas enclosed with fly wire. Holes in the fibro, a rickety front door, back door, and kitchen door covered with fly wire broken in places so the flies come in anyway. The fibro sheeting is so thin there is almost no protection from the vagaries of weather, hot one night, freezing the next. The wind blows in first from the front and then from the back. The rooms inside are dark and bare with no access to outside light. The whole structure sits precariously on this land. In the deep silence of night doors creak in the wind, an empty haunted sound.

We eat outside beside the small glow of a fire that does not disturb the spectacle of stars and planets moving across a vast black sky. The black night around us is soft and smooth, like a warm blanket, and silent. The breeze of the day gone, it is so still and silent, with only the occasional rustle of a night animal in the bushes. Some of the time we just sit in silence, and then there will be the rise and fall of the gentle murmur of voices as we chat about looking for the Narran Lake.

The next day we go looking for the Narran Lake on a property called Terewah, having borrowed the U'Alayi language for home of the black swan. With Chrissiejoy at the wheel we venture through an open gate and follow the tyre tracks to try and find our way through the next gate. We end up driving round and round the original Eighteen Mile paddock of Boorooma following a maze of tracks that could be cars, sheep, or kangaroos. We cannot find our way out of the paddock, let alone find the lake, which seems more and more elusive every time we try.

That night by the same fire the talk takes a different turn. Entering the territory of taboo, a fight erupts between two of the women, each of them angry with the hurts of a lifetime, of generations, of the struggle to be heard. It is an innate struggle between two Aboriginal mobs from the beginning of time that the other Aboriginal members understand, but extremely hard to fathom for the non-Aboriginal members of the team. Daphne storms off into the dark of night and we are all stunned, at a loss to know what to do. It is Daphne's Country but we are miles from anywhere and the nearest mining camp is a dangerous place. Eventually after a night of cars coming and going looking for Daphne, of fear and panic, we are all back at the homestead, fractured and isolated from each other and this place. All night the haunting wind that blows through the old house makes holes in the fabric of my mind.

In the morning, Chrissiejoy takes on the leadership as an Elder in this country and makes a plan to find a way to the lake. She makes some phone calls to local landowners that she knows from her days of living there. After establishing that we are not researchers but a group of artists looking to produce artworks about the Narran Lake, she manages to secure us entry through the fences on the property we had entered the day before which now already seems so long ago. Driving through the same gate we follow the instructions we have been given to find the next gate which we are told is marked with a sign that says "Remington." We are to drive through that gate and then to a third gate that is locked with a huge padlock. Standing beside it is a gruff, nuggetty man in blue singlet and tattoos who grunts at us to follow him. He opens the locked gate and we travel in convoy down to two ramshackle houses.

On the way down, Chrissiejoy gets Badger to pull up in a scrubby area and walks directly to a hidden grave surrounded by a low wrought-iron fence. The man is surprised that she knows exactly where it was, but she explains that she grew up here and this was the Overseer of the out-station of the original property, that her Father had built the fence around it to preserve the grave site. She also explains how and why her friend had died.

The man becomes much more friendly and when we arrive at the two houses, Chrissiejoy can point out to him many original features of the structures including the now converted stable building and how it was originally set up. The man then happily suggests that we can go where we like and leaves us to go back to his own work.

The air blows hot on skin and underfoot is a crackling dryness. Farm litter lies everywhere giving the place a feeling of desolation. One man lives in the house, the other man lives in the workers' quarters. They are the property managers. The house faces what I gather must be the lake, a vast expanse of dry nothingness. We walk down to the edge of the barren expanse and as far as the eye can see, from horizon to horizon, bare dry ground shimmers in a mirage of heat. The mirage looks like water but the drought stricken ground tells otherwise. The man has left us now and we disperse, trying to be present to this barren landscape. I look for shelter, walk over to a small patch of bushes and crouch on the ground in the dappled shade flicking the flies from my face. I notice some tiny bright red fruit on the silver saltbush beside me and pick a few to eat finding them surprisingly succulent and sweet. I feel peaceful beside the red-fruit bush tree surrounded by lake bed and prickles, but I wonder what Chrissiejoy is making of this ghostly specter. Is it exactly as she had feared? We all just leave her be until she is ready to move on.

It is hard to find a picnic spot in this vast dry nothingness but we head around past some dams that were recently placed there, with Chrissiejoy directing Badger where to drive to the other side of the lake, so we can all understand the vastness of the lake. We come to a native willow growing beside a beefwood log; Badger shows us the fine rippled red grain. It is the only tree on the expanse of ridge on the other side of the lake, so it has been heavily visited by cattle leaving dung and many flies. We perch along the dead beefwood trunk and juggle picnic preparations on our small food box as a table, a minute and slightly ridiculous scene in this vast empty space. We eat and joke but as soon as we finish eating Badger says in a low urgent voice, gesturing silently at the ground under the log, "It's time to go." The dead tree trunk is also home for a snake who must not be named for fear that naming will call the snake out to us. We drive back slowly around the edge of the lake past a tiny drainage channel where some tall twiggy gray-brown weed has some green shoots. Chrissiejoy stops the car, hops out, and examines the lignum. We stop to thank the man and give him notice to follow us up to relock the gate and drive out through all the gates back to East Mullane to prepare to leave the following day.

The next morning we say goodbye to Chrissiejoy's country, each of us thanking the place for having us there. Badger brings out his kangaroo skin that he carries with him as a blanket. He shows us the hole where the bullet killed the kangaroo and which he has embroidered around as his Granny taught him. The blanket is made from many patches, each cut into an even shape and rippling with the many different colors of the great red kangaroo. The fur is soft and pliable and he spreads it out and wraps it around himself and me, an embrace of Country and kangaroo. I am grateful for this warmth as we take our leave, still not healed from the events of two nights ago.

Back at home things seem to only get worse. Issues between the two women seem unresolvable and attacks are being directed at me. I feel out of my depth, vulnerable, wounded. I want to run away. I want to think up a different way to do this project, perhaps archival research. It is only by the understanding and words of the other Aboriginal members of the team and deeply contemplating my own long experience of violence that I find the will to go on. I had never understood the origins of this violence in my husband's experience of racism before. There are many versions of this repressed family history. The overall storyline that all others derive from is that my husband's grandfather came to Australia from India and married a young Englishwoman that he met on an ocean liner. They settled in Randwick, in Sydney's eastern suburbs. I wonder now how must it have been for a dark skinned young man to find himself in a fiercely racist and Anglophone white Australian culture? And for the young woman who traveled by boat from her home country in England, leaving all that she knew and loved behind, to have fallen in love with this man?

They had a child they called Frank and the story of Frank's origins was never acknowledged in the family. He looked like Mahatma Gandhi when I met him, an old brown skinned Indian man with his glasses perched on the edge of his nose. There were stories of Frank's violence toward his children when they were growing up, and the Grandmother's violent madness, in little snippets of the Grandparents' lives. My husband's oldest brother inherited his father's dark skin and black curly hair. At school the kids called him Jacky Jacky, a taunt for Aboriginal children, servant-of-no-name. My husband, the youngest son, would stand up for him in fights at school, a punchy little boy looking after his much worshipped older brother. My husband, throughout our lives, had strange episodes of violence as if this repressed story and its effects took over his mind. When I was first able to name this violence, I thought it was about gender. I now understand it as more likely to be the effect of racial violence passed through the generations in the story that could not be told.

> To grieve, and to make grief itself a resource for politics, is not to be resigned to inaction, but it may be understood as the slow process by which we develop a point of identification with suffering itself. The disorientation of grief—"Who have I become?" or, indeed "What is left of me?" "What is it in the other that I have lost?"—posits the "I" in the mode of unknowingness. (Butler, 2004, p. 30)

Some months went by before Chrissiejoy called us together for another meeting in a café in Armidale. She brought with her a painting and a small gift chosen especially for each person. Each gift was something of herself, the lake or the way that team member is now part of her. I remember the painting only vaguely, it is the one painting that has not traveled with me to all of our exhibitions. It was small and the main color was dark, with a circle of bright white stones with people sitting around a fire in ceremony. Through each person's gift she told them a story about their work in the team. The painting was the means of telling another story for us all, this time about the hurts that happened around our trip to the lake. This painting was the traditional way of resolving problems. Chrissiejoy then went on to explain her experience of seeing the lake after such a long time away.

"When I saw the green shoots on the lignum that day at the lake," she said slowly struggling to form her words, "it showed me that the lake is not dead, it is dormant. It is waiting," she told us, meeting us each face to face, eye to eye, each in turn, "and it is our work together to sing the lake back to life."

Map 6: Binnem Binnem Butterfly

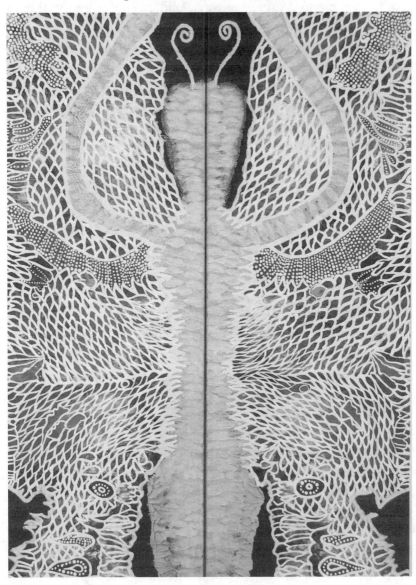

6
A Dry Land

Daphne Wallace[1]

A lot of people were shifted around. I think the idea of that was to break the spiritual connection to the land, that's the way I read it, and then ceremony would stop. All that connection would stop. Mum reckons when she was at Dungalear she remembered the old men going off into the bush painted up. She said she remembered the old men, and after that there were no more ceremonies.

—*Daphne's mother's story, Elizabeth Wallace née Sharpley*

The Midden Painting

I ran into Daphne in the Coles supermarket. We were standing by the fridge where I picked up some yoghurt. "Hi Daphne," I said, "how you going? You want a job working on a project to make paintings about the Narran Lake?" We had just heard about the funding and it was not long after my return from recording Chrissiejoy's stories in Sydney. I explained about the research and that she could respond to the ideas in artwork and stories. "It's like a dream come true," she said, "especially because I'm from out there. I grew up out there, that makes it more exciting 'cause you're from that place."

When you go home you can feel that spiritual connection, when you go back to the place where [there's] proper bloodline connection there. 'Cause so many people shifted outside of their areas that when you do go where your bloodline from you feel it is really strong. At home, I'm so comfortable at home, and when I go other places I'm uncomfortable. [In other places] people say to me, "Oh, you shouldn't be frightened because you grew up in the bush." But our bush had no grass.

Daphne also tells me that her "Mother's been trying to put together a couple of books about bush tucker and she's going out photographing everything." When the emu sign is in the sky her Mum calls her and Daphne makes the thousand kilometer round trip to Lightning Ridge where she grew up to join in collecting emu eggs. Through these stories that the invitation provokes, Daphne quickly establishes her knowledge rooted in relation to Country. The significance of this story is the emphasis on her Mother's documentation, her desire to make their stories visible, through her photographs and art. Through her bloodline, Daphne has the authority to tell the stories of this country, and to make artworks in response to the proposal. On her maternal grandmother's side Daphne is Yuwaalaraay, and on her paternal grandmother's side, Gomaroi.

Mum grew up at Dungalear Station (after leaving Angledool and Brewarrina), halfway between Walgett and Lightning Ridge. It was another big mission or reserve set up and when they were carting people away from Angledool on the back of cattle trucks, like the old Angledool Mission, there was the old one and the new one, 'cause more people went back to Angledool, they carted people on the back of cattle trucks without sides. She said people fell off and they were left behind. The truck wouldn't stop if anyone fell off so people described that as like, they were hanging on for their lives, you know, on the back of this old cattle truck.

They took some [people] to Walgett and then they brought people from Brewarrina and Bourke. Nan (Daphne Sharpley) said if you spoke the language they'd cut your tongue out, this when everyone was rounded up under the Protection Policy and she was only little when that came out and then they used to chop their hands off if they talked like ceremonial sand painting and that. When I first came back here to work in Armidale some property owner brought these photos in wanted us to keep 'em there [at the Culture Centre], and I had 'em out, they just arrived, and then Michael and Doug walked in and they're from the same language group and they just roused on me and then I had to go out and get smoked and got in trouble, and I had to get smoked so bad things don't happen. I shouldn't seen 'em, just one of them things you shouldn't see, but it was the last known, recorded ceremony.

When we were little we didn't fish very much 'cause most of the time you never got a car. There's cars, but if a car did go out some would have to stay behind 'cause it's too many. There's 12 of us, there's seven girls, five boys, 11 of us still alive. I'm number seven of the 12. We grew up down the bottom of Nobbys [hill] at Lightning Ridge in a tin camp. Dirt floors, and when you think about it now it makes you sad to think poor old dad had to cart that water. Yeah, make me realise how strict they were with the water then 'cause we used to get one load, we used to bathe in one bucket of water, like a dish, and so if you were the last one the water was quite muddy. The council had got like, there's still two there today, where you can pull up and fill a tank up with water. It's bore water, and so we had to cart water. Mum used to walk 3½ miles, I painted a painting of this, with a black boiler on her back with the clothes in it and sometimes a baby sitting on it, and wash out at the bore drain.

Daphne came to my office the next day. We organized for her to be employed as a casual research assistant and to record some stories of where she came from. Then she took off for Lightning Ridge 500 kilometers away in Gomaroi country where she grew up. Three weeks later, on her return, she presented me with a small pencil sketch of some middens that she said were at the Little Narran Lakes. Still searching for the Narran Lake and wondering if there was one or many, I asked her to describe where she had been and to tell me some stories. She showed me a whole swag of black and white photos of the middens. The funny thing, Daphne told me, was that for all the time she was at the middens her camera reverted to taking only black and white photos and when she left the color returned. I told Daphne my story of searching for the Narran Lake.

Daphne and I went shopping for art materials so that she could make paintings from her stories and experiences of the trip to Lightning

Ridge. She bought all the sorts of things she could not afford before—oil paints chosen in individual colors and sizes with the colors marked in strips across shiny metal tubes—azure blue, vermillion, emerald green, old gold; bottles of turps, and linseed oil for glazing; creamy white canvases stretched tight on wooden frames ordered in different sizes from tiny to huge; soft pliable squirrel hair brushes and spiky pig's bristle brushes; handmade papers with their slightly uneven texture for drawing and watercolors. Daphne waited impatiently for the canvases to be delivered so she could begin painting.

> They're the best quality canvas you can get, if you can tap on that and it sounds like a drum that's the best, and using the oil, when I get canvas locally they sink in the middle, which is not good, but this is the top quality canvas, so, wonderful, I feel like a real artist, it makes you feel like a real artist. And these are the papers, and them two little boxes that's all the paints, 'cause some of the tubes, like these tubes are $29 a tube. It's wonderful having proper quality. I grabbed some new paintbrushes too and just to have the quality to work with and doin' a painting and having no hair fallin' out of the brush. This is a new medium I'm working with and I'm really enjoying it.

I decided to record the process of art making in Daphne's studio, feeling my way into the documentation of this project. The house is a plain blonde brick veneer in a new estate with a double garage at the end of the ubiquitous concrete drive. The door is double locked, Daphne explains, because of what happened when she was young. Inside the house, another world. Every wall and surface is paintings and artworks. There are woven mats from Arnhem Land, bark paintings, carved emu eggs, Aboriginal paintings in all the different styles, Daphne's and her daughter Alpena's paintings. Daphne took me on a tour of the paintings telling their stories of an elsewhere—other landscapes—the bush, the sea, the desert. None speaks of this suburbia. Here, now.

Daphne's nephew, Frank, is sitting on the sofa, slightly bent over, head bowed, eyes averted, with barely healed bright pink scars marking the skin of his face. Daphne explains in hushed tones that he was bashed unconscious by some Koori lads last week, ended up with 15 stitches and badly shaken up. He shows us, at Daphne's suggestion, a new sketch he has done in a drawing book she bought him, of the "Gura" rainbow serpent story. "He is gonna paint it," Daphne says gently.

Out the back and into the double garage which is her studio— crammed full of paintings and empty canvases stacked along one wall. On flat tables laid out to dry, are the most recent Bubbles paintings, seven or eight of them, wonderful paintings, better than anything I had hoped for. We turn the recorder on as Daphne talks about the paintings, fast and too excited, but some of them have their stories. Daphne's own painting of the Gura, two rainbow-striped serpent bodies coiled on red earth is painted from her mother's story of the rainbow serpents at Lake Corcoran.

> Y' remember I told you when you all was little, what your Grandmother and Darther told me. They were out there behind the Corcorans, lived out there for years, a very long time before the mining started up. Two beautiful Rainbow Serpents, real white skin with rainbow color bands around their bodies. They were very pretty, bigger than pythons, they were there, but not there anymore because of the mining. Yes, they were real, they were there.

A huge oil painting of the flood waters, bright mobile colors, watery movement with the paint flowing over the edges onto the sides of the canvas sits flat on a table to dry. The next painting is a small one of the min min lights, and a story that if you looked into them you never came back. There are two paintings of bubbles on the surface of the river, Daphne experimenting with paint and movement of bubbles and water. There is another painting with a mound of cracked dry red earth under a hot sky; and two paintings of lightning striking the Ridge, in purples with flashes of opalescent white. Then, standing out from all the others, is an oil painting of the middens at the little Narran lakes.

The color of deep red earth pressing into body again under a bright, too blue sky that only such intense heat can produce. A long landscape shape that the eye scans from side to side as it does the wide open spaces of this country. Under the red earth there are swirled layers of orange, gold, and black with scatters of shiny pearl white shells of the

middens, the traces of people feasting on shellfish from the lake for
thousands of years. All shimmers with a kind of vibration, an intensity of energy that I cannot explain. Daphne tells me about the quality
of the opalescent white paint that produces the shell fragments that
glitter in the sunlight. "It's very expensive," she says, "it's made of real
crushed pearl shell." She explains that she's coated the whole surface
of the painting with "linseed fats" because it "brings the color out
more, makes 'em jump off, like jump off the canvas."

> So that's the shell middens runnin' along there, like with the oils it came
> out a different feel, different effect. I can't wait till it dries so you seein'
> it upright but that really blue sky to make it feel like 50 degrees, that's
> why I used that sort of blue 'cause it was so hot that day. And you see
> mirages on the horizon, that's the white line, like little flashes here and
> there of water.
>
> The feeling at that spot, feel like someone watching you, eyes on you,
> that's the feeling, the Old People there, and then we went up to the
> middens, you could imagine everyone sitting down there breaking the
> mussels open and eating 'em, you can imagine it—mothers, everyone,
> children and all that, sittin' down there like this big feast, big feast you
> could sorta see it in your eyes like that, and went up a bit further, I'm
> sure it was the lake but anyway, it feel like they just coming out of the
> lake, the Old People, they're there just watching, makin' sure you don't
> do anything wrong, makin' sure they watch over you.

"That reminds me so much of that dream," I said, "when we were
really frightened at the little lakes. All the people being there." "Well,
that's what we call a visitation," Daphne said.

The next time I visit Daphne she presents me with the midden
painting. It has been exhibited lots of times since and many people
have offered to buy it for considerable sums of money. Even when she
is in financial difficulties Daphne tells me that it is a gift, it cannot be
sold to provide her with money and it cannot be returned. It becomes a
symbol of our work together. The midden painting as gift continues to
connect us to each other and to that place despite the ups and downs
in our relationship. It has traveled with me to the cold forest country
of Victoria, far away from the red heat of the drylands. It hangs on my

dining room wall above where I sit and eat with the people and spirits of this other place. It will travel with me again. The painting as object holds the place, the shared memories and stories, and something of Daphne's "material thinking," a creation that stretches out between us like a thin unbreakable membrane. This membrane quivers through our difficulties and differences, its fabric stretched so fine it threatens to dissolve, but still it endures.

The Yurri Yurri Sequence

During the time of making the artworks for our project, Daphne painted 15 small acrylic paintings to make a child's storybook. The Yurri Yurri book is structured around these paintings, digitally photographed to make the illustrations for the book. Each page has story text above and below the image of the painting in a mixture of Aboriginal and Standard English. The creation of the book was enabled by the project laptop with images and text assembled using the iBook program. Access to these technologies expanded Daphne's repertoire, enhancing her ability to express layers of complex ideas and images in a similar way to Chrissiejoy's thinking through Country. A careful reading of this book reveals much about the hidden meanings of water in a dry land in Daphne's life experience and cultural knowledge. Daphne says the book is about the act of storytelling itself, and about the Yurri Yurri people.

> How this story came about was my mother, Elizabeth Wallace, was talking about the kids and the grandkids are growing up silly these days and mucking up and not doing what they're told and she said it's all my generation not passing the stories down. I didn't think of the story 'cause it was passed on to me [in the usual oral way]. So that's the main reason why I sat down at the computer to type it and in the book I tried to show how it's passed on. There's one other story in the cover also that belongs to out home. Anyway this book is the Yurri Yurri story and it's about the Yurri people that only come out at sundown, after dark, and they take little children away. They take them away for good, never see them again.

The paintings that make up this book depict the changes in the passing on of knowledge in storytelling through the changing practices of home and Country. The Yurri Yurri people appear in every painting as the shadow side of the story that is being told. They are the hidden meanings beneath the story that are only told through metaphor, image, and allusion. In the light of the widespread experience of Aboriginal people of having their children taken away, the last statement that the Yurri Yurri people "take them away for good, never see them again" resonates with the particular terror of this experience. The cover image, however, reveals the paradox within this statement and has strong connections to images of water.

The cover image sets the scene for reading the whole Yurri Yurri story. It shows three figures, Daphne's daughter Alpena with a Yurri figure on each side, "taking her away" across the red earth country toward the stars of the Milky Way. The red earth country in the foreground is dry country ("my country has no grass") and beyond the red earth is the shimmer of the water of Corcoran Lake, the hidden story within the story. The water of Corcoran Lake mediates the figures' passage across the dry red country to the distant line of hills, into the red sunset and the mythical star story of the dark night sky. The movement in this image is from day to night, light to dark, as it is in the book, "'cause most of the pictures are painted, you know, with dark." Paradoxically, instead of a fearful taking away, it is the story of a metaphorical journey through time and place for Daphne's very precious only child, accompanied by the Yurri people, invisible creatures of the other world.

It is the emu-in-the-sky story, "the other story that belongs out home," that calls Daphne to make the 1,000 kilometer round trip to Lightning Ridge to join in the gathering of emu eggs. All of the Yurri Yurri story is embedded in this journey to her home place, her Country. It is the literal and metaphysical journey of her art making and her work in this project. It is also a journey to the home place of language because the book is about language and storytelling. The cover image, then, is about the uninterrupted flow of knowledge and connection that ties Daphne to Country and to kin. It is the flow of the waters. The emu story functions as Daphne's equivalent to Chrissejoy's learning the Mulgury of Country through learning kangaroo—its habitat and habits, all of the things that are connected within its orbit, and how all of this is part of a larger cosmology.

That's how we know the right time for emu eggs, you can tell by the Milky Way. The Milky Way's form it's in. That time of year. Like we never went checkin' what month, we just looked at the Milky Way that tells us it's the right time to get fresh eggs. We used to go out sometimes two car loads, sometimes in the ute, to get eggs. He's sittin on the nest, and when he hears a car comin', they lay down really flat and straight so you can't see 'em through the grass. When you start walkin' across the paddock they get up and run like mad and when you get close to the nest they try to attack you. They usually go for your eyes. So the fastest runner goes across the paddock and the ones not so fast'd sit on the roof or the bonnet and laugh.

You not allowed to touch all the eggs in the nest, you gotta leave one behind. That's because the emu will lay in the same nest the following year, so when you go out hunting you know where to look but if you touch all of them he won't sit back on that egg and he won't lay in that nest again next year if you take them all. Yeah he'll build a nest somewhere else, but also it's like making sure 'cause you want eggs to hatch and more emus for later, more emus the following season, makin' sure there's gonna be enough food there.

One of them would feed the lot of us. There was always 10 or 11 or more livin' at home, and one egg would feed all of us a meal with johnny cake. And, ah, yeah, the bread cooked on the coals. When I was a kid too, Mum used to cook sponge cake out of it, she always argued the best sponge cake [was made] out of an emu egg. But growin' up at Lightnin' Ridge, they never had vegetable shops, see. If you wanted vegetables you had to grow it, and when they stayed out at Carlton Station, they did grow vegetables, but when they moved back to Lightning Ridge, I guess it was too hard to grow in that dirt.

Egg carvin's a big thing now, everyone carves 'em. Like people sought after eggs. There's a young fellow, my cousin Darren down the city, he gave that egg in there to us. He was really young then and now people take eggs to him to carve, and they pay so much money for him to carve an egg. And the other day Mum had, like eight shells, and she took it to him, and she said, "Here, you can have the seven shells, but carve me one." Yeah, like that. And he's a good little carver, he can actually do a portrait of you, like a photograph on the egg. Even when I was a kid we all had a go at carvin' with the shearer's comb. Yeah, that's what a lot of people use. We call 'em dinnamayi and dinnawan gubble, so dinnawan gubble is emu egg, yeah.

This emu story, constructed from its scattered appearance through-out our talk, reveals the nature of the story behind the story. Its seg-ments are told orally, with great speed and a circular rambling quality. Already translated and sanitized in this text, it is quite unlike the linear form of the written word. Every aspect of the story resonates with Country, its very basis directed by a connection to cyclical move-ments of the stars visible in the night sky. It is a story that is always connected to its own representational practices, both in its conscious-ness of the language of storytelling, and in the many stories of emu egg carving. Not only is the egg a source of food and survival but the shell is carved and participates in a new aesthetics and economy of Aboriginal art making.

The journey to enter the cultural place of the emu in the sky story is via the shimmering water of Lake Corcoran. The three figures on the cover go from the daylight image of the dry red earth country through the shimmer of the water to the hills and then the dark of the night sky. Daphne does not tell the story of Lake Corcoran in this book or elsewhere but she paints the Rainbow Serpents that live in that sacred place. They are two white skinned snakes with bands of rainbow col-ors across their intertwined bodies. In the opal country of Lightning Ridge, the Rainbow Serpent is associated with the sacred opal made literally from the ancient underground waters. When Gura was dying a rainbow shone on him and the scales turned to opals. Daphne says that "Just before the drover discovered opals on the ridge, just this side of Lightning Ridge, it's believed that there is an old senior man, Elder man, used to sit there on a rock and he sing all the bad spirits or Gura [opals] back into the ground." These underground stories are held in the shimmer of water in Corcoran Lake which represents the pathway to the deep cultural knowledge hidden beneath the surface. It is cultural knowledge that was once told in a language that became forbidden language and through ceremonies whose performance became punishable by chopping off of the hands.[2]

Each of the following pages of the Yurri Yurri book shows the changing places of storytelling and story over the generations from before white settlement until the present. They are either images of the family scene of storytelling, or the scene of the story itself. After the first one which is prior to white settlement the storytelling scenes are all in the dark of night. This one "shows our ancestors sittin' around a fire tellin' me Yurri Yurri stories, so basically what I tried to do was have it passed on from generation to generation to generation. This is what I'm tryin' to do with the book, so whoever picks up— because our story's verbal storytelling, I try to show that in the painting." In this image the fire is central, it is the only structure of any sort evident on the red ground. There is no camp, the world around is home and country—no walls, no fences, no boundaries, no striations in the smooth space of the field. Only the frame itself, painted into the painting, marks its edges with the specific symbols indigenous to that Country, a reminder that these images are representations not the real, and held within the frame of Aboriginal knowledge.

Daphne claims her home place of oral language and storytelling in typing the Yurri Yurri story onto the page in her version of Aboriginal English: "yerp dar hout dhere eberywair, watching ya." The imposition of Standard English has denied Daphne her natural spoken language all of her life. She has been regarded as "illiterate" and corrected for her way of talking, with no way of representing her knowledge of the world until she finally found a way of expressing her meanings through her art.

> We useda get into trouble, like even off Dad'd go, "Don't talk like your cousins!" (laughs) 'cause we'd spend a weekend—just about every weekend we'd spend in Walgett, whenever we could get to Walgett with Nan and Dartha. An' even if it was for two hours we were there, an' my cousins'd go, "Ooo—look ober der, big numoos ober der, come 'ere big numoos!" Like that (laughs). So, an' we useda talk like this when we was kids. An' my brother was real strong on it up 'ere, like 'e 'asn't changed. I just think it's wonderful that 'e 'asn't changed. When I was workin' at NERAM [New England Regional Art Museum], Joe [Director] asked

me if I didn't mind if 'e corrected me so I could speak so people could understand me. I said, "Nah, I don't mind!" But now I think, I've lost that now. I lost my real strong accent, an' sometime like I know my brother talks a bit silly, but sometime, some of the stuff 'e talks about's really good.

Powerful taboos against the use of Aboriginal languages included the threat of having one's tongue cut out. Even Daphne's father corrected his children's spoken English but somewhere, somehow, Daphne retained a sense that the body knowledge held in the rhythms of this language and its practices of storytelling is "really good." As the book progresses the images of home change from fire to tent to tin humpy to tin shack, "Bit like just sheets of tin, over 'ere it got flasher and flasher, more and more tin." The second page depicts Daphne's Great Grandmother telling her Grandmother, "around a fire, old army tent, sheet of tin," and the third page shows a tin humpy from Daphne's memories of the Namoi Reserve in Walgett where her Grandmother told stories to her mother. The center of the book is a series of images of the tin camp at Nobby's in Lightning Ridge where Daphne grew up. One of my very favorite pages shows Daphne sitting on the floor in the bedroom she shared with her sisters, stars shining through the window spaces, drawing by candlelight.

> I'd be sittin' down scribblin' on somethin'—everyone'd be asleep, candle goin', sittin' on a dirt floor, she'd sing out, "Doesn't 'e go to bed now? Yurri Yurri people in the window there, lookin' at yah. Go right now!" An' you'd blow the candle out an' go to bed. Yeah. I'd be sittin' on the floor, like this is a dirt floor with the white opal dirt 'cause it was harder and mum used to sprinkle water on it and I remember the smell of the damp clay, and we used to share beds and she'd say now blow that candle out before Yurri Yurri woman or man come through the window and get ya, it was always candles.

The final page of the book shows Daphne inside the blonde brick house, woven mat on the wall, sitting at a computer with her daughter Alpena, telling her the story. The text reads: "First time I am telling my daughter Alpena Yuntjai Bronwyn at the computer, she can also pass onto her children and so on," and on the bottom of the painting:

"See Alpena, that how our ancestor, Old People, and our families, passed on the old stories around the fire at night before sleep time." It is the technology of the computer with its facility in image and text that allows the story, with its hidden meanings, to be shared with her daughter in the here and now.

There are only three images of water in the dry country of Daphne's Yurri Yurri story book: the shimmer of Corcoran Lake on the cover, a painting that shows her mother washing at the bore drain, and the image of the Water Dog in the river. The bore drain painting shows the figure of the mother, brown arms and legs in brightly colored dress, stirring the washing in a big black pot over a fire. The ground is bare red earth and through the middle runs the straight lines of the channel of the bore drain with a row of eight brown children playing along the edges of the water. A row of brightly colored clothes is pegged out on a line between two trees, the only vegetation in the painting.

> This one is my mother, an' I've got real strong memories of this 'cause sometimes I think—God you had a tough life. She had an old copper boiler, that was the time when Dad used to drink, but then he stopped drinkin' and he was a good Dad. Sometimes she'd carry the boiler on her back, a baby in it with the clothes, down to the bore drain 3½ miles from where we lived at the bottom of Nobby's. This is the three mile [bore] here and this is the Waterford station where we used to go, but it's not there anymore, bore drains don't have water anymore.
>
> We'd all be down there and Mum used to wash in the old boiler and poke it with a stick and while she was washing we'd be catching our lunch, like yabbies. We used to take a shanghai and knock a bird out of the tree and use the flesh to catch yabbies to eat, and that was our food, and then we'd cook it in a pot and Mum be cooking so we'd sit there and have a feed of yabbies. We'd have to wait while the clothes dried and she'd fold 'em up and put 'em back in there and we'd walk home. Sometimes Dad would drop us and pick us up in the ute [pickup truck]. She used to sing out, now don't wander off you kids don't go out of my sight 'cause the Yurri people will grab ya, so again I think the story was also about our safety 'cause up here there's a lot of mines, like at the top of this red one, so it was a protection thing I guess too. So that story was used a lot when I was growin' up.

The bore drains were constructed to provide water from artesian bores for cattle and for irrigation, bringing to the surface the invisible underground waters inhabited by the Rainbow Serpent. It is now water that is regulated and controlled and the only water that Daphne's family has easy access to. The country and time of Daphne's growing up is dry, with their only regular access to water for washing through the colonized space of the bore drain. They cannot reach the river because they have no means of getting there and they have no running water at their camp. They have to cart water from the Council's communal tap. Daphne grows up in dry country with no access to the flows of water, or to the cultural flows of language, story, and ceremony. And yet the stories remain, hidden in the symbol of the Yurri Yurri people who take children to the land of the stars.

The only place where free flowing water is pictured in the book is in the painting of the Water Dog, the mythical figure that inhabits the special place at the junction of the rivers. In the Water Dog image, the river flows freely with two girl figures walking toward it. It is the place where they went with their Nan, and the text says, "We was not allowed to go near the river, only when fishing with Nan" and "Don't go down dher dhe water dog will get ya, if dhey don't the Yurri Yurri people will." Nan knows the invisible stories of the water so the little girls are safe with her. The Water Dog is a marker for the sacred knowledge held at the junction of the rivers. It is the knowledge of her Grandmother's generation when the waters flowed freely and the opals remained in the ground.

The Binnem Binnem Butterfly Painting

All the while I was recording Daphne making her artworks, my estranged husband was dying. It was like two parallel stories running side by side in my life, my work with Daphne, and my personal dealing with the process of his dying, until the two came together in the Binnem Binnem painting.

I watched, fascinated by the unusual creation of the Binnem Binnem butterfly painting. It was early winter, getting cold by this time, so the painting was inside on Daphne's dining room table. I didn't know the meaning behind its name so I responded to its color and form. The underpainting was made in brilliant rainbow colors on a long thin canvas as tall and wide as my body. The two long thin canvases were then pressed together to make a mirror image, two mirror halves of the same, like printing, making a trace of the other in reverse. "The colors are so joyful," I said to Daphne, "Bright, vivid, wonderful colors, the colors of Spring." Standing at the head of the painting, Daphne touched its surface to show how she worked with the quality of the oils to allow the colors and patterns to have their own life, "'Cause this is like a perfect circle, but then it's got all messed up an' I thought it might stay a bit of a circle, but it didn't." Then I watched the butterfly wings emerge as Daphne added intricate patterns of fine white cross hatching, "All the wings got veins in 'em, well that's what I'm trying to do now, but I'm using all the colored patterns [underneath] to create the veins." I feel a slight sadness, even a sense of loss, as the rainbow colors are slowly and painstakingly overlaid to become something different, something new.

> Lot of work in it. I'm doing all the veins now so it's gonna take me ages 'cause there's a lot of veins runnin' through it. I was gonna use this pearl white but then I decided to use this really white white, and in between you can see the different coloring and patterns, yeah.

My husband died during those ages it took for the butterfly wings to emerge in the fine white filigree veins that shaped their form. The day before he died I sat with him by the harbor where we had first met. I was 14 years old then, only a child. The day we sat at Lavendar Bay we had been separated for some time, a long and traumatic separation, but few words were needed to bring back lives of love and children. He remembered sailing the harbor in boats he built with his father and brothers. During these last months he had talked a lot about building another boat to sail the high seas with his boys, our sons. We sat there by the azure blue of Brett Whiteley's harbor painting to look at a beautiful hand-crafted timber boat that he had watched being built during the weeks of his illness. As he talked with great longing of the boat he would build to sail away, I realized it was his longing for the life he would soon leave behind. It was about the one big unfinished story, the story of my boys, our sons.

He died in the middle of the night, in the tiny flat he rented with his brother for the purpose, so as not to die in hospital. I sat with him on his bed that evening of his last night as he went to sleep and talked to him about my work with Daphne. "It's important work," he said, recognizing my work for the first time, "you must keep it going." I kissed him good night and the phone call came later at 3 a.m. One long gurgling breath, his brother said. I went with both my girls to sit by his side one last time and felt such tenderness for this man, the father of my four children. My lover since I was 18, married for over twenty years, long years of joy and heartache. Such tenderness, and such inexpressible sadness.

Returning home to Armidale I went to visit Daphne and tell her the news. She made a cup of tea and we sat together at the dining room table drinking our tea over the Binnem Binnem painting. She started to talk about my husband, quietly and with great presence. It was as if she called him up to be there with us, Daphne, me, the Binnem Binnem painting, and him. She talked about her lack of education, her illiteracy, of how he helped her to get into college, and then her position as a curator at the National Gallery. She recalled in vivid detail their conversations, laughing at how he used to talk to her. He changed her life, she said, "without his help, none of this would have happened," opening her arms to all that was her life now. Then she turned to the painting. "So this is the body bit up the middle. I did it more like a person than a caterpillar, like with the arms an' that because the story talks about Binnem Binnem people, like Binnem Binnem Butterfly people, not like the caterpillar, like the transformation." Then she told its story:

> Now this is a Binnem Binnem—you know that Binnem Binnem butterfly story? A few years back, I think I was pregnant with Ali, think it must've been about '97. Mum's brother passed away—Uncle Brucie— and at the Catholic church they read this story, the Catholic church recorded the story from Teddy Fields, a local story at a local place at Walgett, on the river, and I painted it because ah, I couldn't get it out of my mind.
>
> The Yuwalaroi people went down the river an' met these wonderful people, the Caterpillar people and they thought they were really

wonderful people and friendly and all that stuff. They did their fishing and everyone got on really well. Then when the Yuwalaroi people went back down the river a few weeks later, there was no Caterpillar people around. An' they thought they had died. So what happened, they turned around and had a big mourning-like ceremony for them, and painted up and that, thinkin' they'd died.

The following Spring the Yuwalaroi people went back down the river again and there was this beautiful people there with beautiful colors. They were the Binnem Binnem people, the Butterfly people. And what the Binnem Binnem people said to them—'cause the Yuwalaroi had all the big mourning ceremony—and they said, "No we didn't die. Our spirit just transformed from that caterpillar into this beautiful butterfly."

I carry the midden painting with me still. It tells me about a hot dry land where the only visible water is in the shimmer of the midden shells painted in crushed pearl shell white. Through the midden painting and its stories I am inhabited by the spirits of that long ago place of middens by the lake. The Old People who visited me there live on in the painting. Daphne felt them there too and told me her story about feeling the presence of the women and children eating the mussel shells by the little lakes with the gift of the painting. Without the certainty of Daphne's story I might have doubted their presence, put them down to an act of imagination, fantasy, or even willpower. The midden painting is a powerful force in staying true to this writing. Learning presence of self to others, to places, and how to express it, is the work of Country.

The Yurri Yurri book teaches me about the invisible stories of water hidden underground in this dry country, the stories that cannot be spoken. The landscapes of colonization in Daphne's world are dry— the cracked red earth of drought, the white clay mullock heaps of the cratered landscapes of opal mining, the painting of lightning strike at the Ridge with no rain. The three paintings in Daphne's body of work that show the flowing of the waters are from the time and place of sacred water. Real water flows in the time beyond memory when the sacred was more than taboo and language told stories of Country.

Map 7: Iron Pole Bend, Wilcannia

7

TRAVELING WATER STORIES

Badger Bates[1]

I'm sitting there sometimes
on the town side of Wilcannia
Ithu, Yuunkuli kulpa kulpa nguku
that means swans flying over
singing out
and water coming down
the Warrego, Paroo, or the Darling
and they going to meet it
that's why I always put the swans
flying overhead in the picture
they tell you where the water's going
over there to Nepabunna, Lake Eyre, Lake Frome.

Mapping the Great Arcs of Movement, Water, and Country

Paakantyi artist Badger Bates and I began our work together in my office with the biggest road map of western New South Wales spread out between us. We wanted to record the special places that Badger will make artworks about so that when he returns to his home in the far west of New South Wales, I will know where he is talking about. The road map is nearly a meter square and extends west across New South Wales into South Australia, north into Queensland, and south into Victoria. The Narran Lake, on the western edge of my known country, is close to the eastern side of this map. It is all remote inland country, with few towns and long distances between them. I am not familiar with any of the words for this country except for a distant memory of the names of the rivers in a voice announcing rising flood levels on the radio in a Sydney childhood. As Badger tells his story onto the map we mark two great arcs of knowledge and movement through country. The first, a continuous green line, maps Badger's travels with his grandmother and relatives to avoid being taken by "the Welfare." The second, a dotted red line, follows the line of water story knowledge, the journeys with his grandmother and the Old People, following the Ngatyis (Rainbow Serpents) as they travel through the invisible underground waterways.

The green line of Badger's journeys of escape by road extends as far south as Ivanhoe, about 280 kilometers from the Victoria border, north to Hungerford just across the Queensland border, and west to Wilcannia, 200 kilometers from Broken Hill. Badger now lives in Broken Hill which is close to the South Australian border, the only regional center in the far west of New South Wales.

> I was a target for welfare, 'cause I had fair skin, blonde hair. Lots of time when we was moving I didn't like it, when I was growin' up, but it was good, you know, 'cause I got to meet people from all over and out Bourke, Wilcannia, and Lake Cargellico. I was getting knowledge off my Grandmother plus these other Old People. My Grandmother was one of my teachers, but also the Old People when I used to go to Bourke, there's Muruwarri people and all livin' around the old mission. There's also Old People from South Australia livin' at Bourke, and from Queensland.
>
> We started from Wilcannia, up to Tilpa, Louth, Bourke, and then down here to Cobar, then Lake Cargellico, Murrin Bridge Mission. Out to Willowra Creek with my old Uncle for a while, back to here on a train, train line there, when you come to there, we'd come on a mail truck or people would come across and pick us up in old cart, old

horse and cart to there, and back to here on a mail truck. Yeah, it was good when Granny used to take me around on the mail truck, we'd go to Tilpa and stay around there for a while, we'd just jump off the mail truck and stay and kill time. And then when we used to go up to Bourke on the mail truck and around Winbar, Uncle Ted and them was there at the Green Hut, and at Yathonga just down from Winbar this way toward Wilcannia, she'd point in there to where the fish traps [were].

The dotted red line of story follows a similar pattern but with a long loop extending east around the Narran Lake. There are also free floating dotted red circles around the Willandra National Park below Ivanhoe in the south, and Warraweena northeast of Bourke, and a continuous red circle with some parallel lines marking the patterns of sandhills made by the Ngatyi over the border into South Australia.

When I was real small, crawlin', just walkin' at a place I's reared up, Gran and them used to work on the dog fence, Uncle Ted, Harold 'n them was always around Brindingabba, Yantabulla, there, come back down here [pointing on the map]. Up in that area around Gundabooka and the Darling River, that's where the two Ngatyi started. They went down through Nocoleche, they traveled through Paroo and Darling National Parks, down to Whitecliffs. They lay around on a hill in Whitecliffs and they created all the land way over to the South Australian border. Then they came back in at Yancannia and Birndiwarlpa where they met the young ones that had come underground all the way from the Paroo. They all went back to the Paroo. The two Ngatyi could change their form into a Water Dog. Sometimes it looks like a big snake and some people say it has gills, maybe it is the male and the female they are seeing. To us the Ngatyi and the plesiosaurus they related so I never—see Whitecliffs—they found a plesiosaur made out of opal. To us Paakantyi people the Plesiosaur is the same as the Ngatyi, you should leave it alone. We were told that opal was left by the Ngatyi and that it is sacred.

That's where it [the creation story] starts, from Narran there, where there's the crocodile, but when I come down [to Paakantyi country], our people say Ngatyi, that's the same story is from there. They took it up around Warrego and the Paroo [Rivers] and down along the Darling, down and up and back again and they brought it back to the country when the ants cleaned everything off. So the meat ants nest, a meat ant on the river, we won't destroy that nest. When we was kids we might go an' torment 'em and run away but we never, we never destroy the meat ant's nest. So they got her back, when they got her back she just about clean and they done it here, but I know that from there it was a crocodile but when it got down into our country it was a Ngatyi that swallowed her, 'cause we didn't know about this thing up here, but we knew the story.

Badger's traveling water stories cross many boundaries of language and Country. There are 18 numbered sites on the road map to indicate the story places for Badger's art. The story places are now marked on a satellite map of country. This large aerial map shows Badger's "really sentimental special place," the thousand kilometer length of the Darling River from Bourke to Menindee. The river appears as the finest black line created by its dotted border of trees. On each side of the line, a ragged narrow margin of gray floodplain, and beyond this the red ochre earth with its myriad pale veins of rivers and creek beds patterned across its skin.

From down there where I went down between Menindee right up to Bourke, that's where is my really sentimental particular place. Also over here on the Paroo, Lake Peery, and back on the Warrego is really sentimental to me, this area, because this is where I lived most of my life, right up to the Brindingabba. But it's sentimental where, more or less in a triangle what I done from Wilcannia, up to Bourke, across to Cobar, Lake Cargellico back to Ivanhoe and back home. And, ah, the thing is the Darling River, that's it, that's me, that's what I love the most, the river and the Ngatyi stories to the river. We call the river Paaka, the Darling, that's how the Paakantyi got their name, the river people.

The migratory water birds traveled the waterways with them and their coming and going signaled other places they had come from or where they were going to in this vast stretch of country. There are many different water birds in Badger's stories—pelicans, cormorants, swans, ducks—but it was the brolga that had stolen his heart. On our first meeting he shaped the air with hands as he told me about a brolga he was carving "standing in the reeds with a baby by her side."

The brolga is like a human because they beautiful and why I'm saying they like a human 'cause they depend on the same things nearly that we, they depend on the water, and the brolga they mate for life. They'll get out and they'll all get around in a circle and have their dances and if something happened to one of them the other one'll come and just put its wings over 'em and cries. That's why us Paakantyi people, even if was hungry we wouldn't kill a brolga, you know, unless we just about dead.

So linking up the Narran and Brindingabba, that's mainly brolga there [pointing at map], that's where they is, but they go there see, and the distance from there to there [Narran to Brindingabba] is not far but look at the distance they have to travel sometime, when they come to visit [Wilcannia] and they go home. Look at that bad distance there, so I wouldn't mind, I don't want to just focus on the people I want to focus on the birds that's getting affected too. When I was only a little fella with Granny, we used to go up that way and see the brolgas dancing on the flat up there. Up towards the station, big claypan on this side of the river. They'd dance around and we used to sit down and watch them for a long time, 'cause we knew they was there and they used to let us go and tell us not to throw at them but just kick back and just watch 'em. They'd danced for us.

Badger learned wood carving from his grandmother and the Old People during their travels through Country. They showed him the scars in the shape of bowls, baby carriers, and canoes, where the Old People had cut timber from the still living tree. He learnt about gidgee, mulga, leopardwood, the trees of the drylands, where they grow, and how to work with the particular qualities of each timber: "You gotta listen, get a feel of it, when I'm carvin' the people that learnt me to carve, old Granny and one of me old Uncles, they just sat and done it by hand." The action of carving connects him to the spirits of the Old People, to the trees and the places where they grow, and to the birds that he carves as they fly the waterways. "Sometimes it's still in the night and the leaves on this kurrajong tree will blow, Granny's here, just do my art work then, wait for the leaves to blow."

When he was only eight years old Badger learned to carve emu eggs from Granny Moysey. The large oval shaped emu eggs are blown and the egg cooked for food. The shells have a dark grainy blue surface, the inky blue black of a midnight sky. As the surface is delicately shaved off, layer by layer, every shade of blue, blue gray and pale gray appears as more of the hard midnight blue outer layer is scraped away. As well as scraping away layers to make different designs, skilled carvers produce images, such as people's portraits, with many different shades of color. It is highly skilled, slow, and painstaking work because of the fragility of the eggshell and it was hard to get Badger to carve the four beautifully patterned eggs for our work.

Badger preferred to use these finely honed carving techniques in the production of lino prints as an art form. The mark making of lino prints is similar to that of carving emu eggs, each imagined and made in the negative image, light on dark, form and color in reverse. Badger has been renowned for his lino prints for many years, producing the illustrations for Debra Rose's *Nourishing Terrains* (1996), her defining work about Aboriginal Country (p. 7). The first of Badger's eight lino print illustrations in Rose's book shows the appearance of his signature symbol, the Ngatyi, the creature of the invisible waterways. More than 15 years later the Ngatyi remains a dominant symbol in his work and has grown in the sophistication of its form and meaning.

His lino print *Iron Pole Bend, Wilcannia*, is a form of "deep mapping," materializing the relationships between country, water, life forms, representation, and structures of knowledge. The print is structured around the two Ngatyis, deeply immersed in the radiating lines of force that represent the creation of the waters. From their mouths the flow of waters bursts forth. Their bodies make the shape of the rivers and the invisible underground waterways in their travels. The flowing waters in the print are alive with the river's creatures—cod, catfish, shrimp, yabby, and mussels. It is a story of the everyday—of the place where Badger's Granny caught their daily food, near where he grew up in a tin hut on the banks of the Darling River and where Granny saw the visible form of the Ngatyi as the Water Dog.

Iron Pole Bend embodies all of the complex knowledge required for catching the river's food and ensuring it is protected, as fundamental to survival. The edges of the water are shaped by the penetration of other mythical creatures whose movement and storylines link to faraway places and storylines. We know these are creation ancestors because their internal structures are visible. The Kangaroo hops beside the shape of Koonenberry Mountain, the special place where the yellow foot rock wallaby became Kangaroo. The Goanna crawls in from its story place in the red sandhills, and the brolga flies over towards Brindingyabba and the Narran Lake. They are passing through from one place to another in one of the water storylines that criss-cross this country.

At the top of the print, in a hybrid combination of a bird's eye view and a more typical Western landscape, we can see Paaytucka, the Moon, and the Emu in the Milky Way. The story of the moon in Lake Paaytucka and the Emu in the Milky Way connects earth country, water country, and sky country, opening the intimate attachments of the everyday and home to the immensity of planetary rhythms of country, water, moon and stars.

The lino print is an image of a different way of mapping, a deep mapping that includes the deep time of creation as well as the present within the one frame. Space, and the way the artwork delineates the spaces and places of these stories, is conceived differently from the way space and place is understood and represented in Western knowledge frameworks. The frame of the print does not foreclose meanings within its square boundaries because the meanings are both allusive and elusive. It points always to connections elsewhere in the flow of water and storylines. The lines of the waters flow in from somewhere else and travel elsewhere. The mythical creatures travel into the frame of the print, but are not bounded by it, they are all in movement.

The meanings of the storylines are *elusive* too, in the sense that we cannot know all of the layers and complexity of these stories. They can be told and represented but they refuse the closure of the already known. As Western viewers we are positioned as other, as the unknowing learner, but the artworks, the maps, and their stories give some access to alternative understandings of water in this dry land. In this we are implicated, mutually entangled in what happens in this place by the actions we take in other places, in our homes in cities, in the urban landscapes that feed from this country. In this print, Lake Paaytucka, the moon lake, is portrayed as littered with dead fish, empty after a decade of drought and no water flows. At the time of carving this print the mighty Darling River had dried to a string of toxic puddles, and water was running out in the town of Wilcannia. Badger says, "So, what I'm up to now, with this artwork, I'm dreaming that the Darling River's in flood, which it's not, but I'm dreaming it's in flood, and it's flowing into the Murray, and that's why all the ripples in the Darling."

Water, Rock and Stone at Peery Lake

In mapping Badger's Country it is hard to stop the flow of stories, birds, and water long enough for me to understand. I need a place to hold onto, to dwell in, and it is our visit to Peery Lake that gives me this. Peery Lake is almost invisible on the whole area of the satellite map of Badger's Darling River, obscured behind the name that marks it as a special place. The closer satellite image of the lake is a body art of country, a vast creamy scapula bone lying over skin of pale red ochre crazed with yellow veins. On the side where the road enters the space of the lake, body fluid seeps yellow ochre from vein and artery into milky white of bone, and on the other, the skin of the land is mottled red-brown. The mound springs appear as clusters of dark dots of trees on the milky white scapula bone. Zooming in to the point of pixellation, the lake is a swirling movement of country, water, earth, color, and form coming into being at this place.

Peery Lake is the place that Badger chose to take us to during our visit to Wilcannia. I remember it in my body and we have lots of photos, writings, artworks now made in response to this stopping place. The trip from eastern Victoria to Wilcannia felt like the same moving whirlwind of places and stories as Badger's mapping. By car to Morwell Station, train to Melbourne, bus to airport, plane to Adelaide, another plane to Broken Hill, and finally drive to Wilcannia the next day. We spent the first day in Badger's old house that he bought at auction for $2,000 to transform into a living artwork of everyday life. That night we sat around a fire under a silver moon in the clearest midnight blue sky.

The next day we set off on the 100 kilometer drive northwest to Peery Lake. The road is red dirt and the country dry with drought.

Badger stops the car at a gnarled tree festooned with a dead looking vine, a bush banana vine, and starts digging at the iron hard soil with a crow bar. As each layer of soil is scooped out of the growing hole, he examines the roots with his fingers. Eventually, he comes to a place where the roots start to thicken and he slows the digging, making small movements along the length of the root. There, deep down and buried beneath the earth's surface is the lifeblood of the vine held in swollen yamlike roots that preserve whatever little moisture is to be found. Wiping off the dirt and moistening the skin of the tuber with a little water we eat into the crunchy nutty flesh. There are no bush banana fruit in this dry season but Badger says the bush banana is an important storyline connected to the Ngatyi. We drive for miles and miles across this dry and barren country in a cloud of dust until the landscape changes into soft dry grasses, small bushes, and more trees where we see birds, more birds, kangaroos, flocks of emus. There are no cattle on this side of the fence in the Paroo National Park, an area of protection established around this last unregulated river.

At the lake the miracle of water stretching from horizon to horizon, in this dry country. As we walk toward the water, stone tools are sprinkled all over the ground under our feet. Emus graze unconcerned a few feet away from us and we share their food, eating the small purple and red fruits from the different bushes as we pass. The water penetrates the land in tiny inlets with shade trees around their edges. Out in the lake, in the middle of this expanse of water, clumps of trees are visible on several little islands. They are mound springs formed by the eruption of minerals in the waters that flow from the springs deep in the underground waterways below. Even when the lake is dry, Badger says, there is still water in the mound springs. Some water just bubbles up to the surface and in other mounds you have to dig to get to the water. Badger walks on alone to a rocky corner of the lake and Sarah points out two piles of rock, one next to where Badger squats down, and another nearby at the water's edge.

Beside these piles of rock Badger traces with his fingers the shape of the engravings barely visible in the flat rock surfaces. Splashing with some water reveals their form—bird prints, roo prints, human foot with long toes, "Clever People," he says. He bends down close, feeling into just how the engravings were made in such hard rock. The engravings follow a line along the lake edge for about 500 meters, most of them now under water. All the little bays in this area are formed by this pink colored rock. Sarah sits on a rock by one of the little bays and Badger watches. He has to keep an eye on archaeologists, he says, or before you know it they will be gone up the hill. On the far side of the lake there are middens, lots of bones, human bones, and a long spit that goes out into the lake with a special pink flowering succulent found only in this one place and at one mound spring in South Australia. Walking back we are told to take a big curve to avoid both piles of rock, rather than walking between them, "so we don't walk in the pathway of the Ngatyi."

> Well there's two lots of stories go into Peery, one's about the two Ngatyi, where they came in, and one's about Kurlawirra, our dreamtime fella, where he got cranky with the people and blocked all the mound springs up. That dreamtime fella, that big fella, he'd done his journey around, through Broken Hill, up at White Cliffs, Tibooburra. At Peery there, when he come back, the people were laughing at him, and then they fed him the lizard and he thought they were going to poison him so he got cranky.
>
> At Peery Lake he grabbed his spear, and they were laughing at his headdress and he got cranky and he jammed the spear into the mound springs, and took his sister and that with him, back toward the Darling, with the water in the water bag, back up to where he come from. When he jammed the spear in the mound spring the people perished and they turned into them boulders around [the lake] where all that old dried mound spring is. When you look at that area it's all dry and burnt and desert varnish on the rocks, you see the fires. You know them big boulders I was showing you where they split, and inside there's a lot of other little stones they put in there, little stone arrangements in the boulders and around the boulders, that's the people what was laughing at him and they perished there. The mound spring dried up, they died of thirst, you know, no water.

The so-called dreamtime stories are the most complex and difficult to understand, even at this elementary level. It is important to stay in a suspended space of unknowing where story, country, image, and body can come together to form shapes of knowledge and understanding. Deep knowledge of Country is learned through these stories which are first told to children and the uninitiated in this basic form. But there are many other layers of story that are passed on through deeper processes of ritual and learning that are carried out through ceremony in Country. In the liminal space of ceremony the forms of dance, movement, voice, sound, body- and ground-designs come together to produce embodied meaning in Country.

> Then he put the Ngatyi in his bag and he went up to where the Darling started, and he met this fella, the Kingfisher, and told him to pull the root of the tree, he's singing the root of a tree and it kept caving in and bendy, and he poured the water in it then, made it bigger and poured the water in and that's how the Darling River came, that started the Darling River, and that why we try and protect the Darling River, us Paakantyi people.
>
> The Mudlark, and also the Ngatyi was in there [the water bag] with the water. And the islands, that's where the Mudlark then see, when he met the Mudlark up there then, the Pee Wee, he formed that island then. That's when he started to build then, there's only a couple around, he's totally different to all the other birds, him and the Twelve Apostle, there's Mudlark, the Pee Wee, he make a nest out of mud, like a mud wasp, and then him and the Apostle bird, Lousy Jack, he makes it out of mud, and the Black Jay, them ones. And so he thought, well I built the river and I'll use the soft mud to build a nest different, it'll be harder, and so it'll be different to any other. So where you see an island, that's where they getting the mud from, because he was bigger [then].
>
> And even today when you walk along the river you see the mud wasp he'll be diggin' and they'll come back to the one place to get the right mud, and he'll dig and take [mud] and make his mud [nest]. And the Mudlark he'll get it, and the swallow too, they'll make mud nests. Yeah, and see around that Redbank, Toorale, Jandara, that's all very special places for Paakantyi people along there, because of the Ngatyi, the Mudlark, you know.

The major storylines, such as the creation of the Darling River, are the ones that are recorded and remembered, but as Gary Williams, Gumbaynggirr elder pointed out, every dot in a dot painting represents a creation story of all the interconnected creatures in that place. Every creature, every living being, has a story in the storylines of creation that connect them to the social realm of language and representation in Country. It is through the assigning of "Mulgury," to use Immiboagurramilbun's U'Alayi language word, that the connection between individual people, groups of people, the beings of the world, and the fabric of country, are formed. In the coming together of all of these elements in ritual practice in Country the storyline becomes a songline. In the ritual of a songline, all of the elements simultaneously come into being each time the ritual is enacted. It is the performance of ritual, the coming into being in the space of the liminal, through which the chaos of the world becomes meaningful, through which Country is sung into being.

This fragment of the story of the mudlark mud is significant. The other birds who build their nests from mud and the everyday life of the mudlark observed by the human is a reminder of the importance of each tiny act of living and its relation to the profound truths contained in ritual and myth. Mud is composed of a mixture of the elements of earth and water, an in-between substance that has deep meaning in the preservation and emergence of new life in a dry country. In the time of creation the creatures were big and the islands were their nests, but each time the mudlark builds its nest, and takes of the mud of the island, it participates in the same processes of creation.

The making of artworks that contain the elements of Country participate in the forces of creation in the same way. Badger made two lino prints of Peery Lake after our visit there. In the first, a daytime image, an expanse of white water with black ripples stretches from edge to edge of the print. Outlined against the water, four brolgas dance and sing on the shore, wings outstretched, fine bird legs bent in movement, heads thrown back in song. They dance on ground dotted with low plants and the long reeds that line the water's edge. Beyond the water a line of hills, and overhead brolgas in flight, long fine necks outstretched in front, long fine legs behind, wings in flight with their characteristic fluted edge of feathers. They fly among clouds floating across a daylight sky, to Bringingabba, to the Narran, a line of flight and story.

In the second, the background is dark, the black and white of the sky reversed, white clouds in a black sky. The line of hills is white not black, and turbulent waters shape the edges of the mound spring. The island of the mound spring is black against the patterns that make the water, and the trees on the island look windblown as if in a wild storm. The water moves with the powerful lines of force of the two Ngaytis that emerge from the waters, both making and being made by them. The Ngaytis' long snakelike bodies with their differently patterned forms of male and female, rise forth on each side of the mound spring, from below the surface of the water, around and above the island mound. Wavy lines of a rainbow join Ngatyi to Ngatyi across the sky above the island. It is an image of the dark, white on black, a nighttime story.

> But with this one, where we've got the two Ngatyi blowing the rainbow, that's because they did come in from when they took their journey from Jandara right around and back into Peery, and that's where the engravings is, where the two Ngatyi come in, the carvings on the rock. This picture's got water in it too because it's our belief that the Ngatyis [are] still with us, and they will make rain, and that's why you always see the rainbow after the rain. We believe that sometimes when it's raining the thunder is the Ngatyi rumbling, growling, and this sort of when they come up and blow the rainbow because they got water now and they can go back, these Ngatyis they can go back on their journeys and people will go there to Peery because water in the lake, and a lot of black people in Wilcannia want to go back up and see the lake full. So with the water, the people are happy, the Ngatyi is happy, and they just really pleased.

Before we say goodbye to Peery Lake, Badger stops in the car facing the great expanse of water and makes a recorded message for Chrissiejoy to bring her with us into this place and then drives us back to Treahna at Wilcannia. On the way back we stop to have a picnic lunch at a dry creek bed with its sprawling white trunked gums telling us that there is water there somewhere beneath its dry surface. Here

Badger chooses some white rock, explaining that it is like the rock of the stone artefacts that we cannot take from Peery Lake. That rock is Ningka, stone that is imbued with the presence of the Old People. They would often camp near Ningka rock in their travels, he says, and Granny would talk to it in language, talk to the Old People whose presence was in that rock. He picks up this white rock and with deft movements of rock against rock splits its surface so that it falls into flakes that lie on the ground. Then in repeated movements of more and more detailed flaking he works the rock till three stone implements are formed, so sharp that they cut through a leaf, through a finger that's held it too close. We took the rock made into implements back to Wilcannia where they were placed on the mantelpiece.

Badger's Wilcannia

Wilcannia feels like a place that is simultaneously crumbling and revitalizing from within. It was established as a busy inland port before so much water was extracted from the river upstream that riverboat traffic was no longer possible. Carved from local sandstone, imposing buildings show the colonial bones of old Wilcannia—post office, bank, hospital, courthouse, gaol, school, police station, church. Most are in good repair, except for the convent, a grand two-story building with one whole wing tumbling rockfall to the ground. Many more recent buildings are boarded up, no longer functioning, despite the fact that in the town's heyday there were 13 hotels. It is Badger's house, and others like it, that tell the story of the (post)colonial rebuilding. Badger says he wants to make his house a work of art and shows us the posts from the back veranda, turned upside down, their rotten ends carved out to make a bowl to hold historic everyday objects found during the renovations. The fence around his backyard is an installation of sculpture and mural.

Ultimately, the town with its grid of streets and houses, tiny on even the most detailed map, is not Badger's Wilcannia. Badger's lino print *Mission Mob and Bend Mob* shows the deep horseshoe curve of the river that shapes the most immediate space of his growing up. The river is marked by the lines of movement of the water and the force field of the Ngatyis within it. The caption says the Bend Mob "lived on the river bank like they always had" and the Mission Mob lived in the Mission Houses on either side of a straight road, "all neatly lined up, all the same with their toilets and showers out the back." Another straight road leads off the road that runs through the Mission houses, ending in a square yard with more square buildings, the school houses. The Bend Mob camps are marked by their relation to river, to One Mile Billabong and the White Sandhill "that belongs to Paaytucka, the Moon." The river with its swimming fish is made by the swirling waters of the Ngatyis, that bursts forth from their mouths. The White Sandhill is lit white by the light of the moon in the dark space of the Mission inside the horseshoe bend. One Mile Billabong is alive with nesting swans and their eggs, water duck, and crayfish. Overhead, swans fly to their faraway places.

Only the mission houses, the schoolyard, and its houses are square, straight, and still, structured in the mathematical form of Euclidian geometry. The road that runs right through the middle, dividing the space into two, ends at the river. The bridge into town is not represented. In the 1950s, Badger was not allowed to cross the bridge into town because his grandmother feared he would be "taken by the welfare." The very last sentence of the caption reads: "My four younger brothers and my sister were all taken away from Aunty Maggie's river bank camp in a big black car." The big black car drove along the straight road and across the bridge taking all of the other children to an unknown world. I don't know what happened to these brothers and sister, but the words echo across the black space of this print held within the curved shape of the river's life.

> Wilcannia is sort of like a horseshoe [shape of the river], from over at Jim Sammons to Yoeval, so we were on one end of the horseshoe and Jim on the other side. Granny reckon Ngatyi hole right through, under the main road, right through from Iron Pole to Union Bend. This hole here, it's a big hole and it never go dry. I'll show you where we was camped one day, and Granny walked outside, we was camped at a tin hut, and no rain but she put her foot down and it was all wet on the top of the bank and she said "look here Ngatyi." When Ngatyi comes from the Steamers Point, that's another bend on the river, it's on that little

map, it changes form and then at Iron Pole it can go underground and come out at Union Bend. That's where Ngatyi live, and we got to protect it, and the cod and them they all go to them big waterholes, the spring'll always feed 'em.

At the Iron Pole, that's where Granny fished, she caught cod and it's where she seen the Ngatyi. Why they call the Iron Pole I think was that years ago, they's gonna put a train line through there and they put a big pole on the side of the river bank. There's a big bend in the river and there's some weed growin' in there, but there was a bare patch there, and it's a stony bank. It's limestone sort of stuff and it's a good place to fish and then also across the river, that's where she seen the Water Dog. One day she was sitting down fishing, sitting there for a long time and getting little bites and she felt something watching her. She looked across and he's just laying there looking at her. And she was talking to it and told it she wanted to get some fish and that, and he never stood up, he just crawled back in the water. She just told it she wanted some fish, and she pulled in a couple of good sized perch and a cod and she went home. She wanted fish to feed the kids.

When I was real small you'd see the fish, they'd come up in the day or night. In the night you'd hear it, this big slap slap, and it was the fish comin' up, chasing the little ones and the tail'd flick, and you'd see them jumping up, you'd hear the big slaps in the night. Moonlight nights was the best time, they'd just go and go and go all night. Sometime you'd hear that real big clap, and Granny'd say, "*Ithu! Parndu thayilana,*" that means "Listen! Cod having a feed." When the river's down I don't think the Nhaampas spawning much, the bony bream, and if there's no Nhaampa the cod he just lay there. When you get water and the fish spawn, then mainly they'll eat the Nhaampa.

In telling these stories of the deep curves, bends, and twists as the river winds around the edges of the town, people are conscious that the Ngatyi is always present in their daily lives. Alive to this world through all of the senses, Granny listens to the cod making its slap slap noise as it jumps out to feed in the night, and she speaks to the cod in language, just as she speaks to the Ngatyi to ensure she catches fish to feed her family. The cod, however, may only be sleeping because cod jumps from the water to feed on the bony bream of the river that only spawn when the waters come down. Every element, including language, story, mythical creature, people, the rocky bank, the water coming down, is a part of the knowledge of Mulgury, the life of the kangaroo or the witchetty grub. Even the silent and hidden, the invisible connection across the horseshoe bend of the river, the underground passage of water is part of this story.

> The billabong was important to get the yabbies, a good place to get the mussels and we was allowed to go there because they knew we were safe. The ducks hang around the billabongs and box swamps. They like them better because there's a thing like a mosquito larva, and that's what they eat. Wood ducks, teal ducks, pink eared ducks, and them shovellors, and swans, and Kuuriilika, them grebes, he don't live in the river because the water move, very seldom swans will live in the river. A grebe he got to have still water because his nest floats. Pelican the same, they live in the river but they don't nest in the river, they got to have still water.
>
> Crawfish, right here near the red sandhill near the billabong here, *mantaalatji* down here and you used see it and you'd walk along and they'd *mantaalatji*, the crawfish go down about a foot, two foot, all the water underneath, and when the mud dry up the sheep walk on it and you see a different round circle like about two foot across, and where you see that you dig right in the middle, it's flat and you dig right in the middle of that different color, Granny used to call that *mantaalatji* and that's where you'll find the yabby. Then push all the mud up and block the hole up to stop the evaporation. They go down in the hole, and that's what you call *maantalitji*, when they push that mud up. So that yabby he'll live down under that ground for months, maybe a year, depending on the moist. And then if he think he's going to die, he'll lay eggs, right, just like fish.
>
> When that billabong get full, where that yabby *maantalitji* in, they'll know when that water rising. He might have had his skin on for 12 months, 18 months, 2 years, he'll come up when all the water all over the place. Then that yabby will shed his skin, and he's very soft and he'll lay around very dopey and that's when you'll see all the cranes and that coming around because they after yabbies. But also that yabby when he come up he'll lay eggs because he's full of eggs. And then the fish go

out and spawn and he's starting to grow, they getting those yabbies with the soft skin, the little baby yabbies. And then you get real small fish, he might be 6 inches or 8 inches long, they good then because they nice and sweet. But you got to be careful of the bones, that's silver perch, black bream, and all that. You got to know how to do it, Granny she learnt me all that. That's why this One Mile Billabong was so special to me when I was a kid, and even now with my artwork.

One Mile Billabong, a shallow ephemeral waterhole, is a place for learning about water. Children are safe there to search for the yabbies and mussels that breed in its shallow waters. Like children, wood ducks, swans, grebes, and pelicans are all safe to make their nests and grow their young in the still waters. When the waters dry and the birds fly away, fish and crayfish bury themselves deep in the mud. Neither land nor water, but both in suspension, mud can preserve both life and the promise of life. In the dry times the crayfish become encrusted in a thick skin burying themselves deep in the mud. The only trace that remains is the slightly darker circle on the surface of the dry ground, a sign of the moisture hidden below. Even before the floodwaters come, their permeable skin senses the coming of the wet and they shed the hard outer crust, in waiting.

Maantalitji is the sign, the dark circle on the surface, it is the animal waiting to emerge with the coming of the water. Maantalitji is dormancy, the liminal of coming into being precipitated by the promise of water. It is through skin, the permeable membrane between inside and out, that the creatures participate in the flesh of the world. It is skin that holds the waiting form of the creature, and that gives way in response to the breath of water when the new form is ready to emerge. "Skin" is the English language term given to the collective assignation of Mulgury through kinship, and "skin name" is an individual's form of this being. It is through taking on the skin of another that a person takes on the identity of that creature—swan, kangaroo, emu, and so on. Skin is the in-between of self and other, the process of becoming other to oneself. Maantalitji is skin and it is sign, it is crayfish, billabong, mud, water, and country changing form, coming into being.

In 2010, after 13 years of drought, the rains came. Badger sent photos of the floodwaters arriving in Wilcannia where they take weeks to fill the great yawning cracks that open up in the black soil plains. Everything that is waiting bursts into life, the grass, the flowers, the birds, frogs, insects.

> See how the water running in here in the Woytchugga channel, now it's runnin' trying to make its way into Woytchugga Lake, what 10 or 15 kilometers from the river, the lake's channel. See how it's running and filling the cracks, this is what I remember when I was a kid we used to sit down near the cracks and watch the flood, and it was a big excitement for us. Well, Lake Woytchugga, it had water in it and we'd get duck eggs, and I don't remember seeing it dry, but then I went away from it too. No water for ten or more years in this channel, but look at it now, it's 50 metres from the fence, cracky ground, this is historic, look at it down here, just running, look. Running in, way under the ground there, pushing down, in the crack there see. All underneath where you is there. If you get here and look down you can see it rippling, that's neat.

He sent a tiny lino print of *The Darling Lily* that springs up with white flowers on the black floodplains after the rain, as a present for my new granddaughter, Lily Jean. The waters kept returning and returning, and in 2011 he produced another lino print of water, *Life Coming Back to Moon Lake*. This time Lake Paaytucka, littered with dead fish in his *Iron Pole Bend* print of three years before, is full of water with cod, catfish, bream, and swans breeding in the lake in a proliferation of new life. The swans are flying overhead telling them that the water is flowing to Nepabunna, Lake Eyre, and Lake Frome, all of the inland waterways flowing with the rains.

Map 8: Baby Cloak

8
CREATION

Treahna Hamm[1]

I've been connected
from an early age
could feel the bond
underneath the soles of my feet.
I was adopted
was back on my homelands
didn't realise how important
until at the Mission thirty years later
saw my Nan's cousin
rubbing the soles
of her great-grandchild's feet
just talking about the importance
of the soles of our feet on the land.

Things used to worry me
wasn't on the right path
but an Aunty used to say
just go down to the river
push your feet into the clay,
it heals you.

The clay is—
so long as there's water in the river
the clay will always be there.

Connection

It is only now, in considering the narrative of my connection with Treahna that I recall that its precondition was to leave my home of Rock and Stone on the northern tablelands of New South Wales.

Armidale May 2006

There are no words.

Only a body sense of where I lie in bed at night in my bedroom—my body in relation to the sound of frogs in the pond below the house, and further down the hill the creek, how it winds from Mount Duval towards the spot where I walk each day, every shape and curve.

Leaving is another failure of belonging.

Gippsland June 2006

I have done bits and pieces of writing but nothing that represents my normal journal. The experience reminds me of Phoenix's *entre deux*— when the world before and the world after are completely different— there is a failure of words. I remember reading this idea in Kay Ferres's article about colonial women's writing. How much more so for them, moving from one side of the world to the other? Perhaps it is simply the quintessential experience of migration repeated from the psyches of grandparents over generations.

Gippsland July 2006

Yesterday I woke in the night with the strongest clearest image of the Gwydir River near where I used to live. I knew exactly which stretch of the Gwydir it was. I could visit it in my body's senses, all the places where we had picnics, lazed in shallow water in summer, camped. But in my dream it was the spot with transparent winding strands of gold on a wide sandy riverbed at the junction of Booralong Creek. We often sat at that little rise and boiled a billy. There were always marks of other fires, of others being there. Sometimes we took food for a barbecue but most often just a billy to have a cup of tea.

Body memory comes as a painful longing that I feel in my heart space as I realize what I have done, how far I have come from the place that has been always there for me, for more than twenty years now, on the New England tablelands.

Gippsland is a land of power stations and brown coal mines where water security means securing water supply for power stations and the water factory recycles water for a city far away. It is a place of rivers, forests, rain, and deep fertile soils where sweet smelling summer grass is cut for hay that sleeps in rounded bales across fields of abundant green. It is where the Murray River rises in the mountains of the south-east corner of the Great Dividing Range as it turns and sweeps across Victoria, forming the southern border of the Murray-Darling Basin. It was here that I met Treahna Hamm, a Yorta Yorta artist of the Murray River.

Gippsland, named for Governor Gipps, is a place of failed male hero stories. Latrobe Valley, its industrial heartland, was built on the labor that produced electricity from brown coal fired power stations. In the 1990s, when state owned electricity generation was privatized, thousands of jobs were lost and the region became characterized by disadvantage and despair. Even more recently, the now international-ized power companies are threatened by the introduction of a car-bon tax and the intense victim story is perpetuated in a new version. Bubbling beneath the surface, however, there are many alternative stories, storylines that extend right across Gippsland and into deep time. These surfaced first for me in an exhibition of women's quilts, a story of resilience, community, alternative economies, the land, a dif-ferent aesthetic entirely. Through my interest in quilts I was connected to Gunnai/Kurnai stories of possum-skin cloak-making in this cold country, and I was introduced to Treahna.

Treahna first joined us on the field trip to Wilcannia, traveling all the way from Yarrawonga on the Murray with three heavy metal engraving plates in her suitcase. I was puzzled because I had always imagined that the artists would be making artworks about their own country. I figured that maybe Treahna was planning to spend some time in Wilcannia on her own work. Then, on the day we went to Peery Lake, she stayed behind to work in the art space in town. When we returned I found Treahna absorbed in etching the shiny surface of the third metal plate, trembling with the excitement of the story of her day in the art workshop at Wilcannia.

Karin came in and she was cleaning up for today. I was talking to her about projects, about remnants and how she collected found objects. She said she'd been doing art for a long time before she started researching, and mentioned she'd done a project about Lake Mungo. I just said, "Look, I'm a Fibrace" and she said my mother's name. I just said, "Oh well, I was taken off her the day I was born."

Karin said "Did you know Yvonne?" I said, "She's my mother. I've only got one photo of her, one remnant." She spoke about meeting my mother and a few other family members and talking about their journey to Lake Mungo and ceremonial experiences there. It was around the time Mungo Man[2] and Mungo Woman were found and their responses to the idea of human remains being studied and researched. Karin interviewed my mother 20 years ago in Cummeragunga, took a photo for the report.

I was taken off her the day I was born and then my [adopting] Mum and Dad came down to pick me up. I've got two identities, two people, two families. I met Yvonne in Sydney in 1992 then came back to Wagga and Uncle Don Atkinson got straight on the phone to family. I only saw her five times and she wasn't in a position to talk about a whole lot of culture because it's all about meeting and bonding and reconnecting. My two main connections to my Indigenous family were through the river and through art. I was drawing ever since I could hold a pencil and I was in Yarrawonga 150 kilometers upstream from where my family was, so it's always been art and the river.

During the day Treahna had completed the engraving of two of the metal plates and when I found her still in the art space she was working on the third. Hands moving in a mobile, stream of consciousness way, she makes line and movement in black bitumen on shiny silver. The first metal plate has an outline reminiscent of the outstretched wings of a bird that Treahna says morphed into the deep horseshoe bend of the river at Wilcannia. The eagle, Badger's totem, symbolizes our arrival to his Paakantji country and the huge eagle that lay spread out on the road when we arrived. Inside the space of the eagle-wings-horseshoe river, are the symbols that indicate Country for Treahna, "looking into the land and seeing things in the land." At each bottom corner six half-circular lines represent the six of us as we traveled together talking stories of Country, "those words, sentences, stories, get woven into the work." Our shared story stitches me into its symbolic forms and offers a depth of interpretation beyond the surface, "There's a lot of unseen connections, and bringing the unseen realm and symbols into the seen world."

The second etching is the ground of Country with its scattered symbols, meanings, and forms. Some images are interconnected, joined together like the moving blue dots in Chrissiejoy's vivid painting of the Narran Lake. Others do not move and merge, but remained disconnected, placed in groups of similar categories of shape and form.

I had a catalogue with me to do with the people from around the Coorong[3] and I was just looking for a starting point. It had to be something to do with fragmentation and remnants, which is sort of like the basis of how we're taught with our elders and just the feelings I've had. So I was looking at a collection of rocks and shells that was in a catalogue and I saw that in an archaeological sense, or a European sense, that a lot of the things were all placed, things that were similar together, like little collections, which is usually what everyone does at home anyway. So it was all about having your individual story and also in another sense, if they're all together and they're all similar, it's like family stories as well. That's why I put groups together which represent bone, stone, and wood. So there's individual stories and there's a collective story of who you are within your own family, but then when it's taken out of context, a land/cultural based context where it's more fluid, which I've put in around these, collections of thoughts or memories, fragments, remnants, it's all joined up anyway.

Treahna's etchings are a kind of body/place journal written in symbols of Country. The image resonates strongly with the experience of the trip to Peery Lake even though Treahna was not there. The stone artifacts, the ningka stones, lying on the ground at Peery Lake were scattered, irregular, joined in pattern and form to the ground where they lay. The stone artifacts that Badger made on our way home and placed in a group on the ground, then as a collection on the mantel-piece in his house, are identical to the grouped stone artifact shapes in the center of this etching-in-the-making. It was when I saw the third etching, however, that I became fully aware of the extraordinary synergy between my memory pictures of Peery Lake and the symbols that Treahna had generated back at Wilcannia.

> This one, after all that happened [meeting Karin], because that was a big thing, I just thought I'd have a play around. So I'm starting to think of my totem, the long necked turtle and I started to do the long necked turtle heads, and I'm thinking oh, that looks like an emu from the back, but then that also looked like a woven bag, and I'm going this is inter-esting, because it's like doing weaving but I'm painting, it's just free thinking and seeing how it all connects like this as well. And then I put the reeds on the bottom, like I would on a breastplate or a bag or some-thing, which can mean the people that live here. It's all connected to the land. I thought that's interesting with the emus because it was impor-tant with me being here in Badger's country and the emus being impor-tant here. So then I put the beaks of the emus there, talking and looking towards each other, and then to depict the landscape, the flat, very flat horizon. The really strong sky. I thought well, looking at the landscape, it's so fragile around here so that's when I started to use the brush work and fine it right down and make these little plants that would have been used to weave with. That's what I'm doing now with this nail.

There is something powerful about the recognition of Country, of meeting country itself face to face in the mutual attunement of these symbolic forms. The bird figures dancing on ground among puffs of grass in front of the lake, the water from horizon to horizon with-out end, is eerily identical to the photos from Peery Lake. It is also so much more than that in the power of offering up the symbols to an audience, inviting them to enter Country. Watching Treahna cre-ate the fine grasses with a nail, etching through the layer of black bitumen into the metal plate, mirrors this process of deep symbolic representation in which the surfaces, the skin of country is every-thing, but its meanings lie beneath in the layers opened up between the body consciousness of artist and of Country.

It's very soft working through bitumen, so what happens it goes into the acid [bath], and I'll work on the fine lines first and then once they're done, work from fine lines to thick lines, so as I go, I'll put these in the acid first. When they're eaten down, then they get covered up, so it's like a reduction print. And then I'll work on the smaller line, right through here, and then they'll get blocked out, and then I'll work on the thick lines back there. So, looking at the plants and how fragile the land is, that's why I used the brush strokes to brush the bitumen right back. I just find the landscape around here beautiful. A lot of people would look and say oh, there's nothing here, they wouldn't be able to see anything, but there's heaps of things to see.

I always don't want to be neutral, because that stops people from, I mean, they see two emus or two turtles there. What I find, the sym-bolism is also in the interactive storytelling and how you uncover lay-ers when you talk to people as well through communication and share experiences. It's the same way as we get taught, we're not given every-thing on a plate. So I like to reflect the experience of how I learn within culture to other people through my work, so that you can see it on one layer, see it on another layer, know a little bit more and a little bit more, and just do it as true to culture, or my way of cultural teaching, that I can. I never set out to do that in the first place, it's just that I was discon-nected from my culture and my family from the start. It was getting in underneath and peeling away that layer, where you see the bones and not the outside of things.

The next morning Treahna and I walk together to Karin's house because she is too nervous to go alone. The house is a little sandstone cottage that looks as if it was once a commercial building of some sort, with a blank stone wall facing onto the street directly opposite the colonial grandeur of the old Police Station. A door on the side opens onto an artist's world of objects, paintings, stories. All the spaces of the house are taken up with artworks in every medium and form with the colors and textures of this place. There is a beginning basket with a tightly woven base in the shape of a vase and then out of the base spring all sorts of grasses with different textures and patterns, seeds, and stalks. Treahna and Karen talk at length about their art making and a little about Treahna's mother. Not many words, the deeper meanings of this exchange carried in the silences between them. Then the handing over, from one artist hand to another, the precious photo of Treahna's mother taken by Karin on those early fieldtrips.

Treahna carries the photo in a small unmarked white envelope as we walk back from Karin's in the strange light of a dust storm. A waist high spinifex roly poly blows alongside us with its intricate lace mesh of fiber all pink with red dust. Everything, our skin, clothes, buildings, footpath, sky, are all dusted a delicate orange-pink. Treahna turns and says, "There's a softness in the landscape through the colors, the pink's very soft even when it's a dust storm. Having a pink sky is pretty incredible." The next day we traveled back to our homes and I didn't see Treahna's Willcannia etchings until they arrived from the printers for our third exhibition. No longer silver metal shining through black bitumen they were transformed with the color of the pink dust of that walk back from Karin's in Wilcannia. They are the color of Treahna's story, of the ground of that country, and of the red ochre designs on my skin in the desert.

Weaving the River

I asked Aunty Yvonne
how to make a turtle
"turn your basket upside down
to make the body."
I've done a lot of turtles
that's reinforcing
my identity to myself
it's not just a turtle
it's my totem
ancestral connections
from the river, the reeds,

stitches mean family
it's the connection the turtle has
between water and land
symbolises family, land, and life.

Fifty women in a get together
we start weaving
everyone so engrossed
we're all talking
the words going into the stitches
of the work

listening out the other side   the smell takes you back
that little turtle could be   to the river
a twenty minute conversation   and the touch,
take that into another work   you can be at the river
into another turtle—   where you belong.

Through her learning from a long line of Aunties, Treahna continues a tradition of weaving the river. Aunty Yvonne Koolmatrie lived
all her life in Ngarrindjeri country, from the wetland wilderness of
the Coorong at the mouth of the Murray River, to the present-day
farming communities of South Australia's lower Murray Riverland.
She has been weaving Ngarrindjeri connection to Country since she
learned from another elder before her, Aunty Dorothy Kartinyeri.
She taught her which plants to use, how to work the plant fibers into
a form suitable for weaving, and the traditional coiling techniques.
Aunty Yvonne Koolmatrie's elongated cylindrical eel, fish, and yabby
traps are woven from sedge rushes in the traditional forms of func-
tional objects used by the Ngarrindjeri people. The technique of bind-
ing a coiled bundle of rushes with a "button-hole" loop stitch has not
only survived, but has evolved since the 1940s and is now used to create new forms. The subtle scent, form, and color of her woven objects,
now displayed in art galleries all over the world, evoke the threatened
environment of the Coorong.

Treahna's totem, the long necked turtle, is under threat from the
loss of water flows in the river. In most years the water does not reach
the lakes at the end of the river. The salinity levels in the lakes have
changed and the young turtles that live there are growing a coral-like
substance all over their shells. Some baby turtles have just a little bit
of the hardened growth, but in others it has completely taken over
their bodies so that they look like a piece of coral. The baby turtles
die because they cannot move their shells, some are not even able to
come in and out of their shells. There is a school in the lower Murray
region where the children go and collect the affected turtles, remove
all the coral growth with extreme care, and then take the turtles up
the river to where it is safe for them to live. Weaving turtle forms from
the reeds that grow on the edges of the river is another way of singing
the turtles, and the river, back to life.

Treahna's turtles, yabbies, and spirit figures woven from the reeds and grasses of the wetlands are the most direct translation of Country into art forms. Watching Treahna pick the reeds, dry them, then leave them to soak in water to soften them for weaving made me realize the significance of the act of making the works beyond the display of the finished product. In the catalogue for the third exhibition of the Bubbles project we decided to document the act of art/place making, so the artists appeared in studios and workshops in the act of making. The materials and tools that went into constructing the works were made visible at the interface between Country and art. We called this exhibition and its catalogue, "The Always Unfinished Business: of Singing the Country" in response to Chrissiejoy's idea that the Narran Lake was only dormant and that it was the work of the project to sing the lake back to life. The catalogue shows photos of the bundles of reeds immersed in water in a tub to soften them, and some beginnings of woven forms soaking again to keep the reeds pliable. For Treahna this act creates a direct relationship to the water of the river.

When I first started the research project, I was at home in Yarrawonga. The river was in the middle where the lake used to be, because it had been drained. There wasn't that many times in my life when I saw the lake drained, usually it was to paint the weir gates or for different purposes, but when I first started this work, there was a sea of green, and it looked like a golf course. I wondered what it was. Usually you'd just see the dead limbs around where the river is, and what it turned out to be was a weed that had invaded the lake and the river. So the local authorities drained the lake hoping that the sun would kill the weed. But what happened was it rained, so it was actually watering the weed, and it was starting to smell, like a bad stagnant smell was coming, emanating from the river, and you couldn't pull the weed out, you couldn't poison it. So it was covered up again and local people were worried because it was almost like a woven mat on top of the mud and they worried about fish and turtles and other things that lived in the water that could have been trapped underneath.

The other aspect was that I started to read through the High Court transcripts.[4] When I started to read, I felt that the questioning was just, there was a lot to do with genealogies but there also seemed to be a lot of time wasting, and the narrative through the court was more directive with the whole situation and the process. It didn't give the elders and community people much of a chance to answer in any sort of cultural depth, because there were things like: "How do you know you were Yorta Yorta?" "Who told you, you were Yorta Yorta," and the Elders would repeat, "My Grandmother, my Grandfather, my Mother, my Father," and the judge would turn around and ask it again. It just seemed to be repetitive time wasting questioning.

I can remember another story, to do with my Uncle, who said that one particular town was where he was told it was Yorta Yorta and he said my wife's buried there at the cemetery and he said, "That's where I'm going to end up." The judge said, "Well why does that happen, why do you want to go there?" And he said "Because if I didn't I'd feel like I was lost" and the last thing that was said to my Uncle was "Is she lost?" referring to his wife. So it was really insulting.

In 2002, the same year that Treahna had connected extensively with her Aboriginal family, she attended the hearing of the appeal against the Native Title ruling that had rejected the land claim of the Yorta Yorta people. In 1998 the claim was dismissed by Justice Olney in the Federal Court who concluded that: "the tide of history has indeed washed away any real acknowledgement of their traditional laws and any real observance of their traditional customs" (Jagger, n.d.). The irony of this finding is multiple and can only be fully appreciated in a consideration of an individual life such as Treahna's. By juxtaposing the impetus of her art as originating in the specific materialities of the degradation of the river system with the Native Title hearing, Treahna defines the issue as being fundamentally about water, about the health of the river. Native Title, and European laws generally, as noted previously, relate to land and not to water because the elemental qualities of water do not allow water to be apportioned, owned, and contained according to laws in relation to land.

In Treahna's experience the state of the river is not an issue that only involves Aboriginal people, but one that affects all people. The community as a whole is "worried about the fish, the turtles and the other things that live in the river." The "community" is not understood as only composed of human beings, but of the elements of water and land, and of the creatures who inhabit those places. For Treahna who was robbed of her Yorta Yorta heritage under European law by being removed from her mother's care, it is a profound contradiction that the same legal system now denies Yorta Yorta claims in relation to her cultural knowledge and inheritance. The final irony is that the judge, in his position of authority and representation of the legal system, uses metaphors of water in his statement that the tides of history have washed away Yorta Yorta culture. Water is the very substance, essential for the maintenance of both culture and life that has been denied to the river and the people. As Simon Schama asks of the Nile, without water, how can we believe in the resurrection?

The question, then, is what response can be made to this "finding" that moves outside these fixed notions of what constitutes evidence, facts, and discourse? How can a bridge be made between a world that is understood in this way and the world of river and flows, water creatures, stories, and genealogies? How are we not to get lost in despair and destruction and with what do we move forward into a different way of being, thinking, and knowing the river, and the world?

> The turtles have to do with the High Court transcripts, whereby one person [is] telling their story. Yeah, like everyone's got a voice in a tribe, everyone's got their stories. There were the elders who told their stories, but really identity is like the long neck turtle, we're one people, that's our tribe, that's what I was trying to get across in that one. So we all move in different directions and the turtle shell's in the background, but, we're one. I wanted to make this big turtle, just to show, you know, when I'm weaving you think about your family, you're thinking about your stories, but just in response, I suppose, to the High Court transcripts as well, to make a totem of our long neck turtle, which would incorporate maybe the different stitches representing the different people in the tribe, and there'd be thousands and thousands and thousands.

The turtle for Treahna is an ontological statement about identity in Country. The very large turtle with its thousands of woven stitches lumbered like the ancient turtles of Galapagos on its platform in the middle of the exhibition, each stitch a person, together making a story, a generation of stories. The baby turtles walked on bits of driftwood around it, smelling of reeds and river grasses. A yabby, standing erect with wavery feelers and eyes of gumnuts, kept them company, fashioned with a quirky humor, the tender humanizing quality of this work. It is the work of forming connections with Country and community, with people and the more-than-human world that Treahna offers through her art, reclaiming the stories from the failed Native Title claim to fashion a new identity.

> So I thought I'd just pick out the Yorta Yorta stories. First of all I wanted to coincide people with artworks, but what I found towards the end was that, there was a whole lot of dialogue within different works that related directly to everyone. So they're all interconnected no matter what mediums they are, and what stories they tell, it's really all about a shared history and a shared knowledge and experiences. So it doesn't matter if I, you know, I didn't grow up at Cummera or I didn't go to school at Barmah, what's important to me when I hear stories to do with community is I visualise my Nan, or her sisters, that did go to school at Cummera, that did live at Cummera, I visualise them through the old photos, because I never met any of them. I've got photos of my Nan's sisters when they were at Cummera, and they were like maybe 7 or 8 years old. There's beautiful little things like that that you get during the research. Photos play a big part in what I do, they help me remember. They don't cut off as much as words do, they're not so, I mean, poetic text is really nice as well, but I like the element of space around things.

Using the photos of her mother's generation, Treahna found a 1950s fabric from a pink and green flowered dress that shaped the deep consciousness of her memory making. From that fabric and its colors grew a whole new lens for the river and its creation. She painted a triptych of three works on canvas about the creation of the Murray River in brilliant pinks and bright blues. Together the three canvases formed a whole but they hang with the small spaces of fracture and fragmentation between them, the generative space of Treahna's making.

For the exhibition we chose a set of three works based on the colors of her mother's dress to hang together on one wall. One is a photo of a yabby woven from sedge grass, its bulging form sitting on the riverbank against the river's pink-tinged sunset reflections. In the middle, the three paintings depicting the river's creation in pink on blue on each side with the creation serpent in deep red on blue in the middle. The third in the set is another painting, a turtle shell erupting into a mass of baby turtles, in delicate shades of aqua and pink. Like Virginia Woolf in her memoirs remembering the flowers on her mother's dress she'd seen as a baby, "I can describe the fish but I cannot describe the stream," Treahna seeks to re-create the flow that is mother, Country, us, all embraced in one. She offers us a view of the world seen through the pink and blue of her mother's dress, a dress that she never saw, that she did not know, "making the links and connections feeds creativity, it just fills the void, it is all to do with the river."

Creation

Baiame sent the old woman
down from the alps
with her stick
and two camp dogs
she walked along
and she created
a line in the sand
and the camp dogs followed
and then Baiame sent down
the serpent to follow her
and he followed the line
she dug in the sand,
which made the bed

of the river
and he sent down the rain,
that filled up the Murray.

She walked from the Alps
right down the river
to the mouth of the Murray
where she fell asleep
in a cave down there
whenever you're there
you can hear the sea
it's the old woman
singing in her sleep.

Treahna etched the story of the creation of Dunghala, the Murray River, onto the soft inside skin of a possum skin cloak. The old woman is a tiny black figure at the top of the line of white winding river as it curves its way back and forth across the cloak between the red and yellow ochre forest of sacred red gums. The red gums stretch out as tall spirit trees to fill the spaces between the back and forth of the river, their branches meeting each other in the center. The serpent with its diamond patterns of red and gold, snakes along the white river's course. At the bottom of the cloak the old woman, no longer a distant stick figure but fully embodied this time, lies sleeping in a cave surrounded by tiny dancing spirit figures. Underneath the cave, along the border of the cloak, two long-necked turtles swim away from each other emitting a flow of white water from their mouths.

Possum skin cloaks were made and worn by Aboriginal people in the colder parts of Australia until the end of the 19th century. They were made from up to a hundred tanned possum skins with the designs of country, clan, and tribal affiliations inscribed on their soft inner surface. After the animals were caught and the meat eaten, the skins were scraped clean with shell or stone tools and pegged out on sheets of bark to dry in the sun or by the heat of the camp fire. The finer tendons of the kangaroo and possum were used for thread in the sharpened bone of a fish or kangaroo as a needle for sewing the skins together. Layers of ochre and animal fat were periodically rubbed onto the skins to preserve them.

Women used the possum skin cloaks by day as a covering across their backs and shoulders and by night as a blanket. They were also used as a sling to carry their babies when walking through country. In ceremonies they were used to reveal one's identity in Country, and women would stretch them across their knees and use them as vibrating drums. People were buried with their cloaks, which is why so few remain today: "You've got the beginning of life and the end of life. The babies were wrapped in the cloaks and the people wore their cloaks right through until the people were actually buried in their cloaks" (Reynolds, 2005, p. 3).[5]

Just 100 years later only two possum skin cloaks were known to remain in Australia, and these were held in the Melbourne Museum. One of them, from Maiden's Punt, Echuca in Yorta Yorta country, was dated as collected in 1853 and annotated: "Designs etched on 83 possum skins rubbed with ochre and fat and stitched with sinew." The other cloak was collected in 1872 from the Lake Condah Mission and depicts, among other symbols, the eel traps of Guntijmara country in southern Victoria. Guntijmara artists Debra and Lee Couzens reproduced the Lake Condah cloak and Treahna and another Yorta Yorta artist, Lee Darroch, worked together to reproduce the Maiden's Punt cloak from drawings made in the Museum. Nothing was recorded about the meaning of the designs so the women learned from archival research and from talking to their Elders. Treahna says it was also a process of creativity and imagination: "I'm not too sure about the designs, but to me it relates to the river, very much like a mapping. That's what it seems like—different areas along the river or special places. The river itself is very prominent in the design [of the old cloak]—the bend in the river" (Reynolds, 2005, p. 33).

The women went on to develop several large projects revitalizing the process of making possum skin cloaks. In 2004 with an Aboriginal Arts Grant from Melbourne City Council they worked with community members to make a series of six cloaks, and cloak-making artifacts, pastel drawings, paintings, dance belts, and possum skin armlets. This very large body of work formed the basis for two exhibitions: "Gunya Winyarr" (women's cloaks) at the Koorie Heritage Trust and "Biganga" (possum skin cloak) at the Melbourne Museum. They then worked with each tribal/language group across Victoria to reclaim the making of the possum skin cloak in contemporary cultural forms. Thirty-five possum skin cloaks were made and subsequently worn by community Elders in the Opening Ceremony of the Commonwealth Games in a contemporary ceremonial Welcome to Country. They were then returned to the communities to be used in local ceremonies. Through the cloak making projects Treahna approached me to continue this new/old placemaking practice, the cloaks themselves functioning as transitional objects, bridging the relational space between us.

As Treahna and I walked together that day in Wilcannia to visit Karin, the crunch, crunch of feet on gravel, her breathing fast with excitement, she told me the story of meeting Karin the day before and hearing her say her mother's name. I thought about baby Eva Luna and how close I felt to Treahna during the time she was born. How I was sitting on the train one day and got a message from my daughter that she had been in hospital all day, they had not let her go home. The placenta had died and begun to disintegrate, baby was at risk. Jes was afraid, I was afraid. I got off the train before I arrived home, turned around and went back to Melbourne to fly to my daughter in Sydney. Eva Luna was born, grandaughter of the moon, my moon baby.

I remember the last time the team met at the airport on our way to Wilcannia when I was again terrified for the life of that little baby. I don't know if I wrote about the day of terror. The day after Jes got home from hospital she calls and says the baby is cold, I cannot get her warm, she sleeps all the time and I can't wake her up to feed. She sends a photo of Eva on her iPhone in a little dark pink woolly elfin hat. I see her face as cold and not-yet-here, her spirit still hovering somewhere between this world and elsewhere. I am afraid for her and for my baby, Jes. At the airport on our way to Wilcannia, I decide I cannot go, I must go to my baby.

Treahna tells me the baby is going to be all right. She gives me her brooch with colored stones for good luck and a book of the Elders so that I carry them with me. She tells me that she, and the other women who travel with us, are the Aunties. She tells me to massage the baby, especially her feet, and talk to her about the birds. The birds are the ancestors looking after us. Take her for walks and talk to her about the birds. She tells me about watching the Aurora Borealis as Luna was being born and when naming her to think of the morning sun, she is Eva, a new beginning.

So, as Treahna and I walk toward Karin's a few weeks later, I tell her how close I feel to her and how it is hard to be cut off from Jes for the first time since all the trauma. I am so bonded to that little baby. How I think Luna is all right now, I have to trust. It has taken me a long time to trust. At Karin's I talk about these connections of my own. Women's business. Treahna talks about working with fragments and returning the fragments to the flow of everyday life in place, to their belonging in the whole. Treahna and Karin talk about their art making. I talk about my art practice as a choreography of people and country, bringing people together, making connections.

It was especially during that time between returning to Gippsland from Luna's birth and going back to Sydney on the day of terror that the exchange between Treahna and me was like a psychic line of connection. It was during this time that the birds appeared. A blue gray heron and a white egret land on the wide ledge outside my office window. They come every day, water birds. Fly in with wide spreading wings that follow the waters and parade up and down the ledge with high water wading steps. Blue gray heron flounces overlay of fine wing feathers and white egret alternately stretches out its long fine white neck shining, then tucks it into feathered shoulder to rest there on that ledge. I photograph them as they walk up and down, wondering where they have flown in from. They seem to be worrying for me. I tell Treahna the story and e-mail her the photos. She texts back that they are the ancestors, the Old People come to look after me and the spirit of baby Luna. It was during this time that Treahna made the baby cloak for Luna.

The baby cloak is made from possum skins found in a neighbor's shed and offered to Treahna at the time of Eva Luna's birth. The possum skins came from around the river, from Treahna's home, before she was born and taken away. They had been in the shed since the time of Treahna's Mum, precious skins because all the other cloaks had to be made of skins from New Zealand where possums are not protected species. I lay the baby cloak beside me now as I do this writing and it holds all the tenderness of that time, the strength of the bond between us.

The fur on the outside is soft and warm, the inside an intensity of color and symbol. At the top in the center an elongated oval shape with a thick outer rim, a pale red ochre womb space. Protected within are the symbols of the ancestor birds, the leaf growth of new life, and a nurturing breast. The womb space opens to a passage lined with the leaves of the ancestors that line the white river in the creation cloak, leaves from the trees of the sacred spirit trees, the mighty River Red Gums that line the river. The passage leads to the bottom of the cloak where it merges into river patterns of moving waters, into the flow of water and of life. Around the womb space at the top and all down each side the white river curves and bends, surrounded by patches of patterns of all the different countries around the river. In and out of the river winds the rainbow serpent of creation. It is Treahna's and my mother-stories in Eva Luna's baby cloak.

Imagine the river
without a map
having it in your head
that's how people
found their way
if they got lost
the little ones would start
with a small cloak
as they got older

they could come along
with it on
just throw it down
and talk with the mob
this is my country
where I come from
you could wear it as a cloak
and use it as a map together.

Map 9: Black and White

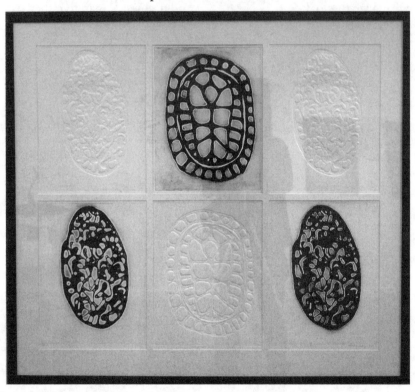

9
MUTUAL ENTANGLEMENT[1]

The river
holds our identity
it holds a lot
of who we are
a lot of our history
and what the Old People
handed down.

How much is
just sitting there
like the seeds
under the ground
waiting to come up
that can't come up
until you start talking.

Our collective story began at East Mullane, searching for water. We circled round and round the Eighteen Mile paddock following sheep tracks in the dusty ground and end in a locked gate. It was that night at East Mullane that things fell apart. We were six people from different countries and crossing the boundaries of those countries into the territory of the other is the hardest thing to do. When I remember this time I think of the solace of the place of East Mullane. The lengthening shadows on the red earth with no grass, the desert trees, the luminous night sky, Badger's dark hands floured white with kneading johnny cakes, the flapping of flyscreens in the deserted homestead that sits so lightly on the land. I think too of Badger's story of the Paakantji people in Wilcannia locating water when the town ran out during the long years of drought, "Where the Ngatyi is, water will be."

It was Chrissiejoy's bringing us together and telling the story of the lake as sleeping that began the long slow process of learning to sing the waterways back to life. We came together in each other's country there at East Mullane near the Narran Lake; then at Swan Hill on the Murray River; and in Wilcannia on the Darling River. In each of these places we talked about our work together as a group and shared being in those places. We planned the process of representing our experiences of water in Country for the next exhibition from these exploratory conversations.

In the transcripts of these conversations, our voices intermingle, each responding to the others' words, until it is not clear who is speaking any more. Stories become collective as different voices contribute to the flow of conversation. I record my impressions at the end of each day, trying to identify the storylines of people together in Country. It is hard to catch the fragments as they float across my consciousness. I wonder if I should just let them go, but I want to make some sort of record of the flow of our storytelling. I write images, stories, bits of conversation, revisiting them over and over to allow something of their collective meanings to emerge. This is my way of learning to sing the other.

Singing the Other: Representation

Turtles, yabbies, birds	try and put Narran Lake here
bringing the river back to life	that's where it all started from
people'll be bringin'	"Memories of Narran Lake"
their fishin' lines in	Narran Lake lino prints,
when you walk into the gallery	and Chrissiejoy's little paintings.

We can create Narran Lake
then bring the Darling down
and that'll meet the Murray,
connecting the rivers
because everyone's got
different creation stories

Paakantyi, Muruwarri, Ngemba
right along the Darling
and even the name
for the Murray River
is different all the way down,
and different stories.

Badger made two lino prints about Narran Lake in response to Chrissiejoy's stories and her suffering. They are his gift to the lake and to Chrissiejoy. The first print, "Memories of the Narran Lake," is his imagining of the lake coming back to life with the return of the waters. Its irregular shape is created in the relation between water and land, the ephemeral waters always land and water both. The Ngatyi flows in with the Narran River, animating the ruffled surface of the water with its force field of energy lines. Black swans and pelicans float on the surface, and fish swim in the water below. Tucked into its curved edges, emerged from their state of dormancy, shrimp and yabbies live amongst the weed with the mussels that clump together there. The brolgas, "human like us Paakantyi people," dance on its shores. They fly overhead too, on their way to Brindingyabba, Yantabulla. And on the other side, emus dance beside a father emu sitting on a nest of eggs. He has his head down when sitting on the eggs, the sign of the emu in the sky, the time of abundance, of feasting and ceremony.

The second print depicts the mythical black swan who was there in the beginning, "It was always *Terewah*, home of black swan, they were part of the lake and the lake was part of them." The mythical swan, with its interior visible on the outside and the outside visible within its body, fills the frame as it floats on the wavy lines of water. Inside the swan are all the creatures of the lake—shrimp, mussels, snails, weed—that provide it with sustenance from the lake's waters. The swan's bones and organs are laid out in symbolic form, and inside the outline of its body, the place where swan meets world, are the typical symbols of Paakantyi culture. The swan is nature and culture as one. Under the elegant curve of its black neck, sheltered in a nest among the bulrushes, is a clutch of nine eggs, the great rush of new swan life when the water returns.

It is in deeply contemplating these two prints of the lake coming to life that I begin to understand. I learn so much of the lake, the swan, and of the renewal of life in the cyclical return of the waters. Face to face with the lake and its creatures, I begin to acknowledge them as part of me and me as part of them in generating the making of these works. As Immiboagurramilbun says in thinking through Country, "You are given a Mulgury at birth and it comes with the responsibility for that animal or plant. Part of that obligation is to learn all about your Mulgury and everything that is connected to it." I have never seen the lake when the waters return. Like Badger, however, I have listened to Immiboagurramilbun's stories, contemplated her paintings, worked with her methodology, and been transformed by the processes of research that led to the making of these images. I have shared the loss, the grieving, and the will to imagine something different.

Our conversations at Swan Hill on the Murray River are about how to bring that different imagining to the world. We wander around all sorts of topics that are prompted by being in that place by the river, and by our planning for the next exhibition. There is one story that seems to hold the meaning of the collective stories of people and water country. It is a story about the Murray cod that once inhabited all of the waterways of the Murray-Darling Basin. Like the map of the Riverine language group, the distribution of the Murray cod overlaps exactly with the map of the Murray-Darling Basin. Murray cod live to a very old age and grow very large, the largest freshwater fish in the world. The creation stories say that it was when a big old Murray cod was caught and cut up to eat, each of the pieces made one of the fish species that live in the waterways. The Murray cod is now threatened with extinction because of the dams and weirs that block their migration.

"If you catch a Murray cod," Treahna says, "it has the map of the tree where the cod was born in its stomach." Badger adds, "When you catch a cod if you take his stomach out, it's white with veins, and if you take it out steady and stretch it out on a piece of white board, you'll see the tree where it was born, leaves and everything." We talk about this image of white on white, of the inside skin that lines the cod's stomach and the fine lines of blood in veins that make an imprint of its birthplace on the white board. We want to create a print of the cod's stomach lining with the blood that flows in its veins. The Murray cod, Badger then tells us, returns to that same tree on the river to die.

At the Swan Hill Regional Gallery Badger imagines Treahna's woven creatures in conversation with his wood sculptures hanging from the ceiling in our exhibition. "We'll have yabbies, turtles, and fish, dangling on fishing lines as if people are walking into the rivers." Badger carves a Murray cod from an old River Red Gum tree. On one side its body is rich red, silky smooth from his hands rubbing and oiling its patterned surface. On the other, a thin covering of metal pressed to make skin of cod, is the glint of cod in sunlight through water. Treahna makes a Murray cod out of chicken wire, woven in parts with reeds from the river. Visible inside its chicken wire body, instead of the creatures of the water that give it food to live, is the rubbish that it eats from the river. Golf balls, plastic bags, bits of fishing line that sometimes cause its death.

My own recurring memory from the Swan Hill gallery is of a print of hanging carcasses of cattle etched in white on a black background with text that says, "Some have lost their ears." This gathers up some of the images from that first visit to the Narran Lake—the amputated collymongle trees, the dead echidna on the road with palms turned upwards, drops of kangaroo blood on red earth from the shooting at the little lake—with talk of bodies, flesh, and making artworks. Badger's deep fleshly knowledge of killing food to eat is interspersed with Treahna's story about collecting road kill with her cousin Maree, stopping every time they see a dead roo on the road. Treahna has to get out and cut off the head with a hacksaw, the head is left to decompose in water in an Aunty's laundry so Maree can use the teeth in her artwork. These conversations gather together in a sequence about kangaroo and possum skin cloaks that begins when Badger shows us his kangaroo skin blanket and Treahna the photographs of her possum skin cloaks.

Badger explains how he buys a tanning kit and throws the skin into an old Simpson washing machine, rotating it two or three times a day.

"You gotta put your hands in to turn it," he says. Treahna shows Badger photos of her possum skin cloaks and imagines the two cloaks—the kangaroo skin blanket from the Darling and the possum skin cloak from the Murray—as expressions of the two rivers. Badger says he couldn't sew the skins together with sinew because "Uncle Col ate my tail." They examine the embroidered detail of the kangaroo skin, "I started on my blanket—I stitched around the bullet hole, and it's sentimental for Granny, so this thing like a boomerang is Granny and me sitting around the fire, and it's her walking stick." Treahna explains how she collected red ochre from the Barmah forest to make the designs on her possum skin cloak.

In order to create a cloak from possum or kangaroo skin the animal has to die first. The kangaroo is killed for eating. The patches of fur stitched together from the big red kangaroo skin change color, depending on what part of the animal they come from, retaining the memory of its body. The fur of the kangaroo changes with the weather, the season, and time of year, "a calendar" Badger says of his life and work. It is an expression of the flood plains of the Darling River country that grows abundant grass after rain. In the process of inscribing meaning onto his kangaroo skin blanket, Badger's beginning point is the bullet hole that pierced the skin of the animal and caused its death. He turns the bullet hole into a circle using the stitches his Granny taught him. The bullet hole circle now symbolizes hearth, home, and country, "It's sentimental for Granny," with Granny and Badger sitting around their campfire by the river. Beside them is Granny's walking stick, carved from tough desert wood and smoothed by her hand, its image now embroidered on the kangaroo skin. The labor of killing, tanning, and stitching creates a new thing from the skin of the dead animal, the embroidered detail telling a story, not of death but of ongoing life.

Treahna touches the deep red color of one of her possum skin cloaks and says, "It's the first time I've ever been to an ochre mine." An old Uncle took her to the ochre in the Barmah Forest and she was surprised when she saw its deep rich red color. The color reminds her of the River Red Gums that grow in the forest by the river, "They're like the spirits of the Barmah Forest—the trees that are sticking out of the land, and all the spirits are down underneath." This is an important cloak, she says, because it is the first time in 150 years that ochre has been used on a cloak. She passes it around the family so the Elders get a chance to wear the ochre from Country against their skin. With her finger she traces the cloak as a map of the river and as the figure of a woman: "The water comes out of her hands and the white in her hair means wisdom. The wisdom goes around her heart and her womb, and the creation goes back into the land like an umbilical cord—in and out, and in and out." The red of the ochre, she says, is the red of the flow of blood in the woman's body, blocked by "all these little locks and weirs, the blood in her body changes direction."

By taking from the ochre of the sacred Barmah Forest, the spirits of the trees are reborn in the cloak. The ochre, as the source of inscription on the skins of the cloak, brings with it the trees of the forest, the spirits of the Old People who dwelled within it, and of the river as the source of life. The skins are the possums that live in the trees of the forest by the river. Together, ochre and skins are the possum cloak's expression of the Murray River. The ochre literally brings something of country to be worn against the skin of a human body, "Wrapped in a possum skin cloak," and is also the signifier for identity and connection in Country. Like the ochre designs on the body in ceremony, in the act of wearing the possum skin, country, creation, representation, and person are made as one. Each time the ceremony or the creative act is performed and shared, each is made anew.

The possum skin cloak that Treahna made for my tiny baby girl participates in the same story of new life. Its soft dark possum skins ripple and glow with the rich warm-bodied fur of the possums that live in the trees of the sacred Barmah Forest by the Murray River. The ochre red of its designs takes its symbolic meaning from Country. It incorporates the symbols of the blue gray heron and white egret of the waterways, the ancestor spirits who came to visit me during the time of fear for the life of that new baby. It both recalls and re-creates the moment of country on skin in the desert; red ochre and touch of fingers, rhythmical thud of feet on ground, and vibration of deep guttural chanting entering body through the red earth, all now gathered up in its presence.

I bundle up the baby cloak to take to our exhibition, "Water in a Dry Land," at Albury on the Murray River. Treahna would not let me send it with the artworks, or leave it at the Gallery for the time of the exhibition. The cloak had to remain with the now-two babies. She said it could only be there while I was there too, for the first few days. This meant that at the opening of the exhibition the baby cloak could be shared with landowners, townspeople, local Wiradjuri people, irrigators, media, and so on, not as an artwork in a glass cabinet (where another of Treahna's cloaks is on permanent display), but as something to be felt, worn, embraced in all of its material presence.

Learning the Other: Art as Public Pedagogy

It's there
that power
that spirituality source
is definitely there
it's a good way.
Who pays homage
to the river?
Who says thank you
for giving us water
to live?

Maybe the wider community
if they saw something like that
people will understand
will be an optimistic thing
to do
a lot of people
would want
to be involved.

This work about water has a life of its own, moving from place to place and project to project. There have been six exhibitions in different locations, each time emerging from our ongoing conversations with each other and the place, and the works that have been produced in response. Each of these places has its own multiple stories of water, always already there, into which our presence and stories are inserted. We have had visitors from Russia, Britain, Sweden, Canada, and the United States too, each bringing something of their own places. Artworks have been bought and traveled to all of these places, carrying with them something of their stories of Country. The exhibitions are the place where the inside meanings of our work together as a team meet with the multiple water stories that others bring. In the exhibition we called *Water in a Dry Land* in Albury on the Murray River, we tracked the processes through which the artworks and their stories open a space of learning to "think through Country" for a public audience.

The story of Albury began in 1824 when the first white explorers ever to see the Murray River arrived in this place. They had set out from Melbourne to find new grazing lands and to expand the search by mapping the western rivers of New South Wales. By 1919 the droughts that threatened the new agriculture on these grazing lands had led to the construction of the Hume Dam for irrigation. The town is a center for the surrounding agricultural communities that grew in response to the possibilities of water from the dams on the Murray River. The exhibition is held in an iconic building of colonization, formerly the Town Hall, now the city's art gallery, a grand two-story sandstone structure with deep arched windows and ornate turrets. Inside, its spacious rooms have polished timber floors and sparse white walls. The ceilings are high and filtered sunlight comes in through translucent blinds on the large arched windows.

The hanging of the works brings other stories of water into this space. Inside the door we hang Treahna's three new works in the colors of her mother's 1950s dress, the dress she never saw. They show the creation story of the river, the totemic turtles, and a woven-reed yabby photographed in the pink of sunset on the riverbank. Next along the wall, Immiboagurramilbun's small paintings of thinking through Country are grouped together, a kind of ancient talisman that carries the energy of Chrissiejoy's Narran Lake. Daphne's oil paintings glow with the intense colors of Lightning Ridge, her dry country of no grass, and a tiny painting of her mother washing with nine kids playing by the regulated water of the bore drain. Badger's lino prints bring his vision of Iron Pole Bend, Memories of Narran Lake, Mission Mob, and Emu in the Sky. His life-sized carved wood birds of the waterways stand in the four corners of the room, flying in from all four directions, in conversation with the artworks on the walls.

There are about 80 people present at the opening of *Water in a Dry Land*. It begins with a "Welcome to Country" by a Wiradjuri Elder from this river place. Aunty Nancy speaks of the river and her attachment to its waterways, first in language and then in English. She welcomes us all as visitors to her country. Dressed in a Wiradjuri possum skin cloak made as part of Treahna's community arts project, the welcome imparts the gravitas of ceremony. Aunty Nancy then asks me to speak on behalf of the exhibition and the artists.

I tell the story of our work together as artists and researchers, beginning with Immiboagurramilbun's methodology of thinking through Country, her intimate connection to the Narran Lake, and her feelings about going back there. "We hope this exhibition will change worlds," I say. I then tell another story of my work with Treahna and the making of the baby cloak. I hold it up, soft skin in my hands, warmth of babies in the story, and invite the audience into its meanings of water. I tell the story of its making, the intertwining of self and other in Country, of new life: "Imagine the river without a map … this is my country, where I come from, you could wear it as a cloak and use it as a map, together." The baby cloak is then placed on a white plinth in the middle of the exhibition space and the audience are invited to experience it.

Many people approach the cloak, hesitantly at first. They look at its inscribed designs, and then start to touch it. They explore the inside skin surface where the designs can be felt as much as seen. They plouch their fingers into the deep soft fur of animal, of possum. I watch all of this and it looks as if they are participating in a ritual of place. Touching identity with their hands, feeling Country with their sensing bodies. Through the cloak as sensory object they are finding a bridge into a different way of knowing. Some of them take photographs of themselves holding, or even wearing, the cloak. Possum, cloak, story, country, person; a moment of coming into being.

On the next day there is an "Artists talk" when people can come and meet the artists. Badger and Treahna rearrange the chairs around the central plinth, reshaping the square space into a series of concentric circles. In the center of the circle the white painted plinth is occupied by Treahna's woven turtles—the giant turtle, each stitch representing one of the Yorta Yorta turtle people, and baby ones walking on driftwood. Overhead the Murray cod hangs suspended with its chicken wire form filled with rubbish. Treahna and Badger sit within this circle, separated by the fact that they are seated on an antique colonial chaise longue. The artworks on the square white walls are a still backdrop to the dynamic space of people and conversation.

An older woman begins, anxiously searching for words, hesitantly speaks her story into the space of the circle. "I am a landowner and farmer, my family has lived here for generations. I love this land, every tiny part of it." She says she tells stories of her land over and over to her grandchildren because she does not want them to forget. "People need to know their stories," she says, "know their history." When she goes to meetings about the weirs that block the flow of the waters, she gets distressed because she has no words to say. "Next time I will tell them what Treahna says, that the weirs are clots that block the blood flow of the river." Treahna responds to her, and to the assembled white audience, "There are so many interconnections through the land itself, seeing the land like a natural human body, kidneys, blood flow, weirs like blood clots."

The artists listen deeply and respond to all the audience stories, their hesitations, stammerings, and questions. The conversation flows from the space of the exhibition with its artworks and stories, to larger questions of caring for the environment, climate change, the fate of the earth, and the relationship of all of this to global indigenous knowledges of place. Together we make a collective story. The final conversation is about the importance of cultural flows. A Wiradjuri woman talks about the importance of flows of water to the flows of Aboriginal cultural knowledge. This idea sits for a while in the space of the circle, the white audience temporarily silent. Then Badger responds, handing the story back to them, "Cultural flows are not just for the black people." he says. "You should all talk about cultural flows because there is advantage for the lot of us, for everybody. Get behind us and do it. It is about time we don't see this as black or white and see one Australia. White people came here a long time ago too. We all drink the same water. We want you to get behind us and support cultural flows."

Storytelling creates the line along which knowledge flows. It is both content and process. The storylines are about the mutual entanglement of bodies and places, about our love for our places, the illness and well-being of people and of country, the caring and healing of bodies and country, and the making of artworks for the renewal of the waterways. Through the exchange of stories we all become immersed in creating a collective material, emotional, and spiritual storyline of thought in Country. The artists tell stories about their places and placemaking through art; the audience tells stories about their attachment to their local water places, their concerns about the waterways and the environment, and their desire to hand on stories and places to the next generation. The stories flow from one topic pause to another, beads on a string, making new storylines of water and water places.

The body is the vehicle, the means of carrying the flows of water knowledge. The materiality of our human bodies is linked to the body of places and their well-being through the performance of the exhibition. The materiality of the body is shared through the possum skin cloaks, worn in the Welcome to Country ceremony, presented to the audience to touch as the baby cloak artwork, and told as a map of the river to be worn. It is the physical and embodied act of making the artworks that connects the artists to Country. The trace of that *making* resides in the works and it is the material traces that, in turn, connect the people who are viewing the artworks to the country of their making. The artworks, as body, are also material objects with a life of their own. They are purchased and circulated to different people and places. They are given as gifts both within and outside the project, carrying with them the body traces of the country of their production.

The space inside the circle where all the different stories come together to clash, separate, merge, or grow into new knowledges, is the place of our mutual entanglement in water. The audiences at the exhibitions are invited into the circle of the contact zone, opening up a space where previously silenced and invisible stories and histories can be told and heard. It is an invitation to enter a different country. The space inside the circle of chairs created by the artists is a powerful signifier of a contact zone where an audience can hesitantly put their words and wonderings. It is a space of uncertainty, of openness, of half formed ideas, of stammerings, of the inchoate, the not yet thought. This is the necessary beginning point for making new stories, for singing the Country.

Becoming-Other: Transformation

That's the beauty
of working in groups
and communities
you get inspired
there's dialogue
between people
not only people
but between artworks
you can see a good way

to talk about
how you feel
or what you want to say
in your work
it's starting to reach out
right through country
cross over boundaries
and cross over cultures.

Treahna's work, *Black and White* is her gift to this theorizing. A large fine black frame holds six separate prints, three on the top and three on the bottom. In the center at the top is a black and white image of a turtle shell, the shell of the long necked turtle that lives in the waters of the Murray River. The black and white turtle is Treahna's totem, it is Treahna, it is Dunghala the river, it is land and water together. It is the turtle whose shell gets so covered with coral-growth that it cannot move, the turtle that needs the flow of healthy waters to survive. On each side in the bottom set of three, there are two emu eggs printed in black and white, forming a triangle with the black and white turtle shell in the center at the top. The emu egg is a symbol for Badger, it is Badger's emu country, it is the emus dancing at Peery Lake, and the emu in the night sky who tells the time for feasting and ceremony.

On either side of the black and white turtle in the top row is the white on white of an embossed print of an emu egg. Tactile and embodied, an embossed print can only be seen in the shadows made on the surface by the raised portions of the white paper that have been pressed into the indentations formed by the carving of the design. They are the shadow side, the hauntings of the story. They are the spirits of the Old People who hover in this image, all of the emu people. In between the two black and white emu eggs is the shadow presence of the turtle people in a single white embossed image of a turtle shell. This image is for the spirits of the Old People, the skin people of the turtle, human-becoming-turtle, hovering in the shadow presence of this tracing.

The large fine black frame holds the three perfectly balanced black on white prints, the turtle shell and two emu eggs, within a large space of white. It is the frame that enables the artist to borrow from the chaos of the world, taking from the life force of creation. These are also held in perfect balance by the three white on white embossed images, the shadow story of the black on white prints. The six prints themselves have no inner frame but their space is separated only by the white line of their edges, so the whole inner text of this work is of the three very striking black on white symbols within a large amount of white space. Only by moving in close do the other presences of the embossed tracings become visible. Then, across the surface of white, in the photograph of *Black and White* from the exhibition, is the almost undetectable shadow of my reflection on the glass, slightly off center, taking the photograph. Each person who stands in front of this work to enter into the space of its subtle meanings will have their reflection cast over its surface.

Thinking through the visual images that these artists have created helps me to find words to name the complexities of working together in Country to produce new knowledge about water. Not only did we create alternative artwork and stories, but those artworks and stories are the site of articulating our own entanglements and the possibilities of knowledge production. Without this entanglement no new knowledge is possible. Each of us moves to the very edges of our being, takes on a new skin, in the process of doing this work together.

When Daphne went out to the Narran Lake in search of water, she came back with a sketch of the middens at the little lakes in the Narran Lakes Nature Reserve. Her experience echoed my dream of the people camped around the lakes, the dream which was my only comfort in the terror of a night of shootings. Daphne's vision came through an act of imagination from stories she has heard all her life about the shells that remain from the Old People eating there by the water. Dream, imagination, and reality are one, "A visitation," Daphne says. She came back with a small sketch on a page torn from a project book drawn in ink and lightly colored in pencil at the midden beside the little lakes. After we bought new oil paints and canvases, this sketch materialized into the powerful midden painting.

The midden painting was the first one produced within the work of this research. It portrayed the heat and dryness of the country in its brilliant blue sky and deep red earth. It shimmered with the traces of water in the shells of the midden painted in pearl white literally made from ground pearl shells. The shine of the pearl shells represents the trace of the once alive waters inhabited by shellfish. It is produced from the inside of the shell's skin, smooth and shiny from living in its watery place. It also represents the trace of the Old People who sat by the lake feasting on the shells when the water gave them food in abundance. Daphne then gave the painting to me as a gift that was beyond exchange, carrying all of the reciprocal obligations to Country that I then carried with me to other places. Our sacramental contemplation of the Binnem Binnem butterfly painting at the time of my husband's death brought Daphne and me face to face, in recognition of our mutual entanglements in the other, and in the lost water of this story.

One shared story, the emu story, flows throughout like the invisible waters of the underground waterways. It emerges at times to make bubbles on the surface in conversations, stories, and artworks, shaping our shared histories. The first emu story was there in the very beginning with Immiboagurramilbun's memories of hunting for emu nests in the lignum on the lake when the lake dried back. It was Daphne's first story of how the sign of the emu in the sky calls her to make the 1,000 kilometer round trip to her home in the country of no grass to collect emu eggs with her family. Daphne painted the emu in the sky on the cover of the Yurri Yurri story book, "The other story that comes from that country." It depicts her only child, Alpena, being taken away by the Yurri Yurri, across the red dirt, through the water shimmer of Lake Corcoran to the emu-in-the-sky-land of the Milky Way. In a deeply ironic move, the intense trauma of the removal of Aboriginal children is recast as a return to language, story, and country through water.

Badger connects sky country to earth and water country with the black space of the emu among the white stars of the Milky Way in his lino print *Iron Pole Bend*. This image of the intimate space of Badger's home camp beside the Iron Pole bend in the Darling River is shaped by the Ngatyis, the creative force of the living waters. It is interpenetrated by the storylines of all of the creatures who inhabit that country—kangaroo, goanna, brolga, and emu. The dancing emus on the shores of Peery Lake appear mysteriously in Treahna's etching, even though she wasn't there. The emus in the etching shape-change between emu and turtle—Badger's and Treahna's country in one symbol—dusted red-pink with the ground of country. Then, in *Black and White* we have two emu eggs complementing the single black and white turtle shell, and three shadow tracings of emu egg and one of turtle shell, white on white. Two countries, two peoples, in dialogue, "The seeds/ waiting to come up/ until you start talking."

At times our emu stories turned to emu egg carving. Daphne tells us about her cousin in Sydney who carves. Her mother takes him eight shells and he carves one for her in return. Carved emu eggs are prized and valuable objects. Sarah tells the story of an old Paakantji man who carved emu eggs in the 1870s and who had his occupation described as "Emu Egg Carver" on his death certificate. Badger tells us about learning to carve emu eggs from his Grandmother as a young child. His story starts with the struggle of their daily lives in the new context of colonization.

"When I kicked off,' he begins, "we had to make our own toys, and we mainly, just about every black fella around, survived from a rubbish tip, because sometimes you get food, sometimes you get material to build a house and stuff." This time of the primal struggle to survive, of finding food on the rubbish tip, is also a time of creativity and learning. He began to make his own "toys and stuff out of tin" and continues to recycle timber and metal waste into sculptures today. It was the time he learned to carve emu eggs too, "And then, when I got up to about eight—that's when Granny learnt me how to carve emu eggs." He learned from the Old People, but it was his Granny who was "the boss" of emu egg carving, the mark making that gave birth to his lino prints. "She learnt me how to hold the pocket knife—and I just go from there."

Moved by these emu stories, and always feeling my way into this work, I ask Badger to carve me some eggs for our next exhibition. He looks at me astounded that I could ask him to do this, calls me "Boss," and tells me that carving emu eggs requires a very special sort of patience and concentration. They are so easily shattered in the carving. Badger usually reserves the word *boss* for his Granny. In our conversations about carving emu eggs he evokes his Granny's authority in me, but also plays with the muted but still potent spaces of colonization. He says he'll have a go to remember his times with Granny sitting in the river camp learning to carve.

I talk about our emu stories with a Gunnai/Kurnai research student in Gippsland when the same storyline appears in his work. I had thought of emus as only belonging to the open grasslands of the outback. I ask him if emus once lived in Gippsland and he says they lived everywhere. The emu story lives in the stars, it is one of the big storylines that cross the continent. Then a clutch of emu eggs appears in the most unlikely of places, a second hand stall at the local People's Market in the nearby town of Morwell. They sit in a battered cardboard carton among a collection of old garden tools, a pile of vinyl records, bantam chooks in cages, and other bits and pieces, looking lost and abandoned.

I gently pick up one of the emu eggs with two hands, thumb and little finger of each hand only just meeting on either side of the cool hard shell. Each egg has only one hole at their widest end, so they were not collected for eating. Around each hole is a number etched in fine white paint, as if they are categorized as museum pieces. I have never held an emu egg before. It is cool and dense, midnight blue, almost black, the color of the night sky in Wilcannia. They are finely speckled with a lighter color, like the stars in the deep blue-black sky. Looking closer at each lighter speckle I recognize it is an absence of color with an indentation exactly the same irregular shape as the white on black mark of Treahna's emu eggs in *Black and White*. It is as if the print is a tracing of the shell itself.

I buy a large twiggy emu-sized nest loosely woven with intertwined sticks from an artist in Gippsland in anticipation of the carved eggs. I arrange the clutch of emu eggs in the twiggy nest and wait for the carved emu eggs to arrive. Badger travels to the exhibition in a big old four-wheel drive truck, big enough to house all of the creatures carved from wood to line the imaginary waterways. Each of his framed black and white lino prints are packed in their own individual boxes made for the purpose of the journey. In the cabin, too precious to ride in the back, are three carved emu eggs. The carved eggs are marked with the characteristic lines of Badger's prints, the lines of mark making that he learned from his Granny in carving emu eggs. The carved eggs are in delicate shades of blue, from the palest blue-white through light aqua and blue-grays on a background of star speckled blue. On each side of the eggs are the creatures of the land and waterways whose storylines travel through his Paakantji country—the goanna, echidna, kangaroo—and the rainbow serpent, the Ngatyi. "Where the Ngatyi is, that is where water will be." The carved emu eggs are placed in a glass cabinet beside the twiggy emu nest made from the lake's lignum in the exhibition we called the *Always Unfinished Business of Singing the Country*.

It is the memory of the emu nests in the lignum that haunts Immiboagurramilbun's provocation to sing the lake back to life. The lignum is a ubiquitous plant, a weed for graziers who consider the lake as a site for cropping. Twiggy and useless for grazing cattle, it is also the skeletal frame, the material substance that supports the nest. In its turn, it is the nest that supports the new life that emerges from the eggs. Chrissiejoy says that the lake needs the lignum and the lignum needs the lake to survive. The lignum is crucial to the new life that comes in the cyclic drying back and return of the waters. Her image of the lake as a dead body after an autopsy is of all the lignum ripped out. It is the almost invisible shoots on the lignum still growing in the dry lake bed that signal the continuing presence of invisible water. The green shoots hold the promise of new life, and the possibility that once again there will be emu nests in the lignum by the lake. When the waters return to the dry barren lake bed, the lignum will once again thrive to make nesting places for the thousands of migratory birds who will also come with the waters—brolgas, swans, ducks, pelicans—that fly overhead in Badger's prints.

The emu egg symbolizes the birth of new life from the egg, the provision of daily food, and the cycles of feasting and ceremony made possible by the coming of the water. The carved emu eggs carry with them the transitional story of the Old People, of the liminal space between the time before and the time after the arrival of white settlers in this land. It is the space in which Chrissiejoy's methodology of thinking through Country was born with its need to articulate the unknowable in the space between painted image, oral story, and written text. There are no words in a liminal time and space to tell the changing story of Country. The always unfinished business of singing the country re-creates the death of the old and the coming of the new, in the cyclical return of the waters. The emu stories and artworks are a storyline of us in Country, traveling to each other's countries, making stories in conversations, actions, connections, and artwork, the work of making and the work of singing the waters into being.

The collective emu story was born in the struggle of our time at East Mullane. I remember our emu conversations on the last night there, sitting out by the fire, Badger, Daphne, Chrissiejoy, Sarah, Phoenix and me, talking about emu eggs. "Always leave two," Badger says, "It's cruel to take more, the father emu comes back to the nest and there are no eggs there." Ever pragmatic, Chrissiejoy says, "If you take them all they won't lay their eggs in that nest next year, there will be no more babies to grow up and lay more eggs." "One egg fed a whole family," Daphne tells us, "scrambled, with johnny cakes." Listening to all this, I lie on the table looking into the vast night sky for the black emu shape in the white star sea of the Milky Way.

POSTSCRIPT

Always Unfinished Business of Singing the Country

March 3, 2012

As I come to the end of this writing I am in a new place learning new country, Country of the Darug peoples. I have left another homeplace, again a university refugee. I choose a house in the furthest corner of western Sydney at Emu Heights, said to be named by explorers for the emus that once grazed there. "Welcome, Emu Girrl," the convey-ancers say. The house sits between bush and river on the very edge of the fastest growing region of Australia. There are 1.9 million people in this region from more than 170 different countries, speaking over 100 languages, 35% recently arrived from overseas. Feeling the global flows of people and place. I am also getting to know a new river.

Clambering through thick undergrowth just a few hundred meters from the new house, the Nepean River dances and bubbles as water meets rock and stone. Further upstream, out from Mulgoa, walk through sandstone country to Rock Lookout, the river is silver ser-pent winding through dark tree-filled gorge thousands of meters below. I surf the river on the net to where it turns east and becomes the Hawkesbury, following its wavery line of blue until it swells into the waters of Pittwater around Scotland Island where I had my first two babies. It enters the sea at Barrenjoey, Sydney's northern most headland, just past where we camped with grandma and granddad in a big white canvas tent, my small child self sliding down huge white sandhills.

The Nepean River is Sydney's water supply, threatened during long years of drought. Last night, six hours ago, the waters from War-ragamba Dam were released as the dam overflowed its capacity and the gates were opened. People were waiting at the dam since last Thursday. At 7 p.m. just before it was shown on the news, the dam reached 100% capacity for the first time in 14 years. The dam gates are opened at midnight and the water rushes over its wall. This morning instead of being a quiet presence only audible from the sound of millions of frogs coming with the rains, the river roars. I listen in wonder; it is unmistakably the sound of the river, not the noise of traffic which sometimes blows on the wind, but a body sound of surging water, of movement and energy.

I burst into tears. I have wondered about the irony of finishing this book about water in a dry land in a time of flooding rains. Here in my new place, in this February leap year of my arrival, 21 days out of 29 are wet. It is an all-time record that breaks the 13-year drought in which this book came into being. Aboriginal knowledges of country, however, embrace far more than this brief period of time in this old dry land. It is knowledge that is far deeper and longer than that, knowledge on a geological timescale. The story is also about so much more than literal water. It is about water as flow, movement and transformation, water as culture, and about water in life and death. It is about grieving what we have lost as well as finding the water that is already there.

The tears are for the embodiment of this new river. The loss of the old, the inevitable movement that seems to be a part of my life and my work that takes me to another place, to learn again to attach, to belong. It is a learning that cannot happen until the old is fully acknowledged and grieved. Every day I walk to the river at the end of this little corner of suburbia where bush meets river. I watch the river swell until waves of brown silty water flood dark trunks of casuarinas. A riverside seat is first stranded then submerged, landslides of earth, rock, and stone tumble across roads, and creeks crash noisily toward the river along every fold of land.

The time of the flooding rains was also the time of opening another exhibition that grew from the flows of this work, Badger's *Kurnu Paakantji Country.* The flyer for the exhibition arrived in the mail with the black and white image of *Life Coming Back to Moon Lake Wilcannia.* The white frame of this image is filled with the unmistakable brain shape of the Moon Lake. Its shape is made by wavy lines of the water's edge, the indefinable space where water and land meet. Inside, the water is fine diamond shaped patterns of white on black, simultaneously lines of water and lines of Paakantji culture. The Murray cod, the catfish, and the black river bream swim in its water-culture lines beside circles of white with black spotted centers, the jelly substance of fish spawn waiting to hatch. Black swans float on the surface of water beside clutches of eggs held afloat in twiggy nests. In the red earth, below the water filled lake, the Darling lilies have sprung into bloom, and long necked swans fly overhead. In the top right corner, a flying swan's black silhouette is lit by the great silver moon that shines on the waters when they return and gives the lake its name, Paaytucka, Moon Lake.

NOTES

Acknowledgments

1. Aboriginal language names are oral and belong in Country. Chrissiejoy asked that we preserve her spelling of the language name *U'Alyai*, which has been standardized to *Yuwaalaraay* in linguistic scholarship. Language names vary throughout the text according to the wishes of the speaker. In all other cases standard orthography is followed.

Chapter 1

1. For digital images and text for this chapter refer to http://innovativeethnographies. net/water-in-a-dry-land/mapping-territory.
2. Funded as several consecutive research projects, including "Bubbles on the Surface: A Place Pedagogy of the Narran Lake" (Australian Research Council 2006–2009) and "Water in a Dry Land" (Myer Foundation, 2010).
3. ARC funded project M. Somerville and W. Beck "Connecting the Dots" (2000– 2003), in collaboration with Yarrawarra Aboriginal Corporation and Murrbay Aboriginal Language and Culture Cooperative.

Chapter 2

1. For digital images and text for this chapter refer to http://innovativeethnographies. net/water-in-a-dry-land/white
2. *Aunty* is a term of respect used to designate older women in an Aboriginal community with whom one is in a familial relationship. It derives from the practices of a social organization based on generic kin relationships.
3. NPWS interpretive sign at Collymongle Scarred Trees, Collarenebri.

4. Fibro is a building material, an asbestos cement sheet (ACS) once widely used in Australia and now banned.
5. Language group names have been taken from http://www.environment.gov.au/ heritage/places/national/brewarrina/information.html

Chapter 3

1. For digital images and text for this chapter refer to http://innovativeethnographies. net/water-in-a-dry-land/thinking-through-country
2. Chrissiejoy has asked that her Aboriginal name, Immiboagurramilbun, be used in the text where it refers to her Aboriginal knowledges. She has similarly asked that the term *Aboriginal* be used rather than *Indigenous* and that her own spellings of language names be maintained.
3. Aboriginal language names have been translated into written forms in many different versions. In my own written text I use standard AIATSIS orthography (e.g., Yuwalaayi) but in Chrissiejoy's text I use her preferred spelling of U'Alayi.
4. Noongaburrah, meaning "the water people" refers to a particular clan group who lived around the Narran Lake and spoke the U'Alayi language.
5. Spirit. In a footnote in her Glossary, Immiboagurramilbun explains that "Mulgury" is typically translated as "totem," derived from American Indian cultural practices. Like most translations of complex Aboriginal concepts she believes this is inappropriate and reductive.
6. Niddeerie is past, present, and future and it is with us always, often referred to as "dreaming"; however, *dreaming* is not a word Immiboagurramilbun relates to in her world.
7. Ticalarnabrewillaring is Immiboagurramilbun's Erinbinjori Grandmother's name, and the date of translation, 1961, indicates the depth of translating of these ideas by Immiboagurramilbun, which is Chrissiejoy's Erinbinjori name.
8. Turning something from "spirit," as in the beginning, to part of us, to our reality, our life, our place.
9. *Body/Landscape Journals*, Somerville, 1999, pp. 11–12.
10. Niddeerie has been translated into English from words in many different Aboriginal languages that express this concept as "the dreaming." As with "totem" it is a crude and reductive translation because there is no English approximation for this complex concept.
11. The rail trail is a walking track between Boolarra and Mirboo North in Gippsland where the original logging railway line has been removed to make a commons walking track.

Chapter 4

1. For digital images and text for this chapter refer to http://innovativeethnographies. net/water-in-a-dry-land/literature-review-water
2. Lorina Barker, a Muruwari woman who lives in Armidale, was enrolled in a PhD program with me, and we recorded her stories at the intersection of our work.
3. Although Lorina named the creator, Baiame, in her story, others asked that the creator not be named. The act of naming, saying the word out loud, they told me, is to call up the spirit and power of the creator. It is an act of respect not to say the name; and there is also the danger of diminishing the power of the name by too frequent repetition in inappropriate circumstances.

Chapter 5

1. For digital images and text for this chapter refer to http://innovativeethnographies. net/water-in-a-dry-land/intimate-intensity-chrissiejoy-marshall
2. Language name of respect for Grandmother.
3. Beginning of time.
4. Lignum is a hardy plant adapted to the hot, dry floodplains of the Narran Lakes system.
5. Spelling variations due to translation of oral language into written form.

Chapter 6

1. For digital images and text for this chapter refer to http://innovativeethnographies. net/water-in-a-dry-land/dry-land-daphne-wallace
2. Daphne's Nan, Daphne Sharpley, née Dool told this story.

Chapter 7

1. For digital images and text for this chapter refer to http://innovativeethnographies. net/water-in-a-dry-land/travelling-water-stories-badger-bates

Chapter 8

1. For digital images and text for this chapter refer to http://innovativeethnographies. net/water-in-a-dry-land/creation-treahna-hamm
2. Mungo man and Mungo woman in this conversation refers to three prominent sets of fossils found in Lake Mungo, New South Wales in the World Heritage listed Willandra Lakes Region between 1969 and 1974. They are the fossils of the earliest human inhabitants of the continent of Australia believed to have lived between 68,000 and 40,000 years ago, during the Pleistocene epoch. The remains are the oldest anatomically modern human remains found in Australia to date.
3. The Coorong is the estuarine environment at the mouth of the Murray River in South Australia, the most dramatically affected by the loss of flows of water from upstream in the system.
4. Treahna is referring here to the recorded interrogations of Yorta Yorta people in relation to the Native Title claim over Yorta Yorta land.
5. I am indebted to Amanda Reynolds for the book, *Wrapped in a Possum Skin Cloak: The Tooloyn Koortakay Collection in the National Museum of Australia* (2005), in which she has gathered together this information for her work with Treahna Hamm, Vicki Cousins, and Lee Darroch.

Chapter 9

1. For digital images and text for this chapter refer to http://innovativeethnographies. net/water-in-a-dry-land/mutual-entanglement

REFERENCES

Adams, W., & Mulligan, M. (Eds.). (2003). *Decolonizing nature: Strategies for conservation in a post-colonial era.* London, England: Earthscan.

Altman, J. (2004). Indigenous interests and water property rights. *Dialogue, 23*(3), 29–34.

Appadurai, A. (1996). *Modernity at large: Cultural dimensions of globalization.* Minneapolis: University of Minnesota Press.

Australian Institute of Aboriginal and Torres Strait Islander Studies. Our Languages (AIATSIS). (n.d.). http://www.ourlanguages.net.au/languages/language-maps.html

Barlow, M., Dyer, G. Sinclair, P., & Quiggin, J. (2008, August 30). *Parched: The politics of water.* Paper presented at the Melbourne Writers Festival; broadcast ABC Radio November 21, 2008. Retrieved from http://abc.net.au/nationalinterest/stories/2008

Bates, B., & Martin, S. (2010). *Following Granny Moysey: Kurnu Paakantji stories from the Darling, Warrego and Paroo rivers.* Canberra, ACT: Australian Institute of Aboriginal and Torres Strait Islander Studies.

Blair, S. (2001). Travel routes, dreaming tracks and cultural heritage. In M. Cotter, B. Boyd, & J. Gardiner (Eds.), *Heritage landscapes: Understanding place and communities* (pp. 118–127). Lismore, Australia: University of Southern Cross Press.

Bonahady, T., & Griffiths, T. (2002). Landscape and language. In T. Bonahady & T. Griffiths (Eds.), *Words for country: Landscape and language in Australia* (pp. 171–189). Sydney, Australia: UNSW Press.

Brunckhorst, D. (2000). *Bioregional planning: Resource management beyond the new millenium.* Amsterdam, Netherlands: Harwood Academic.

Brundtland Commission. (1987). *Our common future.* New York, NY: Oxford University Press.

Butler, J. (2004). *Precarious life: The powers of mourning and violence.* New York, NY: Verso.

Carter, P. (1987). *The road to Botany Bay: An essay in spatial history.* London, England: Faber & Faber.

Colebrook, C. (Ed.) (2012). Extinction. Retrieved from http://www.livingbooksaboutlife.org/books/Extinction.

Deleuze, G., & Guattari, F. (1987). *A thousand plateaus: Capitalism and schizophrenia* (Vol. 2, Brian Massumi, Trans.). Minnesota: University of Minnesota Press.

Escobar, A. (2001). Culture sits in places: Reflections on globalism and subaltern strategies of localization. *Political Geography, 20*(1), 139–174.

Ellis, C., & Bochner, A. (2002). *Ethnographically speaking: Autoethnography, literature, and aesthetics.* Walnut Creek, CA: AltaMira Press.

Ferres, K. (Ed). (1993). *The time to write: Australian women's writing 1890–1930.* Ringwood, Victoria, Australia: Penguin.

Findlay, M. (2007). River stories: Genealogies of a threatened river system. *Futures, 39,* 306–323.

Geertz, C. (1973). *The interpretation of cultures: Selected essays by Clifford Geertz.* New York, NY: Basic Books.

Gibbons, R. (n.d.). *Entanglements: The great Australian land war and its effects.* Unpublished manuscript.

Gieryn, T. F. (2000). A space for place in sociology. *Annual Review of Sociology, 26,* 463–496.

Goodall, H. (2002). The river runs backwards. In T. Bonahady & T. Griffiths (Eds.), *Words for country: Landscape and language in Australi*a (pp. 35–51). Sydney: UNSW Press.

Goodall, H. (2006). Introduction [Special issue, Fresh and Salt]. *Transforming Cultures eJournal, 1*(2), x–xx.

Griffiths, T. (2002). The outside country. In T. Bonahady & T. Griffiths (Eds.), *Words for country: Landscape and language in Australia* (pp. 222–244). UNSW Press.

Grosz, E. (1994). *Volatile bodies: Towards a corporeal feminism.* Sydney, Australia: Allen & Unwin.

Grosz, E. (2008). *Chaos territory art: Deleuze and the framing of the earth.* New York, NY: Columbia University Press.

Gruenewald, D. (2003). The best of both worlds: A critical pedagogy of place. *Educational Researcher, 32*(4), 3–12.

Haraway, D. (1988). Situated knowledges: The science question in feminism and the privilege of the partial perspective. *Feminist Studies, 14*(3), 575–599.

Harding, S. (1986). *The science question in feminism.* Milton Keynes, England: Open University Press.

Horton, D. R. (1996). *Aboriginal Australia wall map.* Canberra, Australia: Aboriginal Studies Press.

Immiboagurramilbun (Marshall, C.). (2005). *Calling up Blackfella knowing through Whitefella magic* (DVD doctoral presentation). University of New England, NSW, Australia. Later revised as DVD *Thinking through country.*

Jagger, K. (n.d.). Yorta Yorta native title case. Retrieved from http://www.findlaw.com.au/articles/1293/yorta-yorta-native-title-case.aspx

Ladson, T., & Finlayson, B. (2004). Specifying the environment's right to water: Lessons from Victoria. *Academy of Social Sciences, 3,* 19–28.

Langloh Parker, K. (1897). The origin of the Narran Lake. In *Australian legendary tales: Folk-Lore of the Noongahburrahs as told to the piccaninnies.* Retrieved from http://www.sacred-texts.com/aus/alt/alt07.htm

Mahood, K. (2008). Listening is harder than you think [Special issue, Reimagining Australia]. *Griffith Review Edition, 19,* 163–177.

Malkki, L. (1992). National geographic: The rooting of peoples and the territorialization of national identity among scholars and refugees. *Cultural Anthropology, 7*(1), 24–44.

Merleau-Ponty, M. (1962). *Phenomenology of perception.* New York, NY: Humanities Press.

Murray-Darling Basin Ministerial Council. (2001). *Integrated catchment management in the Murray-Darling Basin 2001–2010: Delivering a sustainable future.* Canberra, Australia: Murray-Darling Basin Commission.

Oates, C. (2011). *Place subjectivities.* Presentation at Space Place and Body Spring School Intensive. Monash University, Gippsland, Victoria, Australia.

Oestigaard, T. (2006). Heavens, havens, and hells of water: Life and death in society and religion. In M. Leybourne & A. Gaynor (Eds.), *Water: Histories, cultures, ecologies* (pp. 94–105). Crawley, Western Australia: University of Western Australia Press.

Pearce, F. (2006). *When the rivers run dry: Water, the defining crisis of the twenty-first century.* Boston, MA: Beacon Press.

Prescott-Allen, R. (2001). *The wellbeing of nations: A country-by-country index of quality of life and the environment.* Washington, DC: Island Press.

Pretty, J., Adams, B., Berkes, F., de Athayde, F., Dudley, N., Hunn, E., ... Pilgrim, S. (2009). The intersections of biological diversity and cultural diversity: Towards integration. *Conservation and Society, 7*(2), 100–112.

Rautio, P., & Lanas, M. (2011, April 8–12). *Aesthetic literacy in relanguaging rural everyday life as good enough.* Paper presented at the Annual Meeting American Educational Research Association (AERA), Round table: Sensing Place: Embodiment and Aesthetics in Ecological Inquiry, New Orleans, LA.

Reynolds, A. (2005). *Wrapped in a possum skin cloak: The Tooloyn Koortakay collection in the National Museum of Australia.* Canberra: National Museum of Australia Press.

Rose, D. B. (1996). *Nourishing terrains: Australian aboriginal views of landscape and wilderness.* Canberra: Australian Heritage Commission.

Rose, D. B. (2000). *Dingo makes us human: Life and land in an Australian Aboriginal culture.* Oakleigh, Victoria, Australia: Cambridge University Press

Rose, D. B. (2004). Fresh water rights and biophilia: Indigenous Australian perspectives. *Dialogues, 23*(3), 35–43.

Rose, D. B. (2007). Justice and longing. In E. Potter, A. Mackinnon, S. McKenzie, & J. McKay (Eds.), *Fresh water: New perspectives on water in Australia* (pp. 8–20). Melbourne, Australia: Melbourne University Press.

Schama, S. (1996). *Landscape and memory.* New York, NY: Random House.

Sheller, M., & Urry, J. (2006). The new mobilities paradigm. *Environment and Planning A, 38,* 207–226.

Shiva, V. (2002). *Water wars: Privatisation, pollution, and profit.* London, England: Pluto Press.

Sinclair, P. (2001). *The Murray: A river and its people.* Melbourne, Australia: Melbourne University Press.

Sinclair, P. (2008, August 30). In M. Barlow, G. Dyer, P. Sinclair, & J. Quiggin (Eds.), *Parched: The politics of water.* Melbourne Writers Festival; broadcast November 21 2008, ABC Radio. http://abc.net.au/nationalinterest/stories/2008

Somerville, M. (2006–2008). *Bubbles on the surface: A place pedagogy of the Narran Lake.* Australian Research Council (ARC).

Somerville, M. (2007). Postmodern emergence. *International Journal of Qualitative Studies in Education, 20*(2), 225–243.

Somerville, M. (2008a). Re-thinking literacy as a process of translation. *Australian Journal of Language and Literacy 32*(1), 9–21.

Somerville, M. (2008b). *Bubbles on the surface: A methodology of water.* Refereed conference publication. Australian Association for Research in Education, Brisbane.

Somerville, M. (2010). A place pedagogy for "global contemporaneity." *Educational Philosophy and Theory, 42*(3), 326–344.

Somerville, M., & Perkins, T. (2010a). *Singing the coast.* Canberra, Australia: Aboriginal Studies Press.

Somerville, M., & Perkins, T. (2010b). Connecting the dots. In *Singing the coast* (pp. 188–222). Canberra, Australia: Aboriginal Studies Press.

Somerville, M., with Wallace, D. Bates, B., Barker, L., & de Carteret, P. (2006). *Bubbles on the surface: More than a catalogue.* Armidale, NSW, Australia: University of New England Printery.

Sondergaard, D. M. (2002). Poststructural approaches to empirical analysis. *Qualitative Studies in Education, 15*(2), 187–204.

Strang, V. (2004a). Aqua culture: The flow of cultural meanings in water. In M. Leybourne & A. Gaynor (Eds.), *Water: Histories, cultures, ecologies* (pp. 68–80). Crawley, Western Australia: University of Western Australia Press.

Strang, V. (2004b). *The meaning of water.* New York, NY: Oxford University Press.

Strang (2006a). Aqua culture: The flow of cultural meanings in water. In M. Leybourne & A. Gaynor (Eds.), *Water: Histories, cultures, ecologies* (pp. 68–80). Crawley, WA: University of Western Australia Press.

Strang, V. (2006b). Turning water into wine, beef and vegetables: Material transformations along the Brisbane River [Special issue, Fresh and Salt]. *Transforming Cultures eJournal, 1*(2), 9–19.

Thoms, M. C., Markwort, K., & Tyson, D. (2008). *Changing channels: Life on the Narran.* Canberra City, ACT, Australia: Murray-Darling Basin Commission.

Tuhiwai Smith, L. (1999). *Decolonizing methodologies: research and indigenous peoples.* New York, NY: Zed Books.

Ward, N., Reys, S., Davies, J., & Roots, J. (2003). *Scoping study on Aboriginal involvement in natural resource management decision making and the integration of Aboriginal cultural heritage considerations into relevant Murray-Darling Commission programs.* Canberra City, ACT, Australia: Murray-Darling Basin Commission.

Weir, J. (2008). Connectivity. *Australian Humanities Review, 45*, 153–164.

White, M. E. (2000). *Running down: Water in a changing land.* Sydney, Australia: Kangaroo Press.

Woolf, V. (1989). *Moments of being.* (J. Schulkind, Ed.). London, England: Grafton Books.

Zalasiewicz, J., Williams, M., Steffen, W., & Crutzen, P. (2010). The new world of the anthropocene. *Environmental Science and Technology, 44*(7), 2228–2231.

INDEX